MW00526741

Religionless Christianity

Religionless Christianity

God's Answer to Evil

Eric Metaxas

REGNERY
FAITH

Copyright © 2024 by Eric Metaxas.

All rights reserved. No part of this book may be reproduced in any manner without the express written consent of the publisher, except in the case of brief excerpts in critical reviews or articles. All inquiries should be addressed to Regnery Faith, 307 West 36th Street, 11th Floor, New York, NY 10018.

All scriptures are taken from The Holy Bible, English Standard Version®, copyright © 2001 by Crossway, a publishing ministry of Good News Publishers. Used by permission. All rights reserved.

Published in the United States by Regnery Faith, an imprint of Skyhorse Publishing, Inc.

Regnery® is a registered trademark and its colophons are trademarks of Skyhorse Publishing, Inc.®, a Delaware corporation.

10 9 8 7 6 5 4 3 2 1

Library of Congress Cataloging-in- Publication Data is available on file.

Print ISBN: 978-1-68451-550-9
eBook ISBN: 978-1-68451-581-3

Cover design by John Caruso
Author photograph by Josh Del

Regnery Faith books may be purchased in bulk at special discounts for sales promotion, corporate gifts, fund- raising, or educational purposes. Special editions can also be created to specifications. For details, contact the Special Sales Department, Regnery Faith, 307 West 36th Street, 11th Floor, New York, NY 10018 or info@skyhorsepublishing.com.

Visit our website at www.regneryfaith.com.
Please follow our publisher Tony Lyons on Instagram @tonylyonsisuncertain.

Printed in the United States of America

Contents

INTRODUCTION

We are in a war. Of course, at its heart, it's a spiritual war. We who call ourselves Christians are called by God to fight in that spiritual war, which expresses itself in innumerable ways all around us, so that what is fought in the heavenlies by angels fallen and unfallen is also fought in our own world, by us, in time and space. God gives us who are made in His image the wonderful and terrible privilege of taking part in eternal things within the context of human history.

Which raises the question: Where are we in human history?

In America we are experiencing our third—and likely our final—existential crisis. The first was our Revolution, when the threat was from without; the second was our Civil War, when the threat was from within. But now we face a third trial, whereby evil forces aim to steal our freedoms and national sovereignty via a globalist world system dedicatedly at war with the God from Whom we derive our principles of "liberty and justice for all," as well as with the principles themselves. And the threat to us now is from both within and without.

This book is a sequel to my previous book, *Letter to the American Church*, which draws the unavoidably chilling parallels between German Christians' silence and inaction in the 1930s and the silence and inaction of American Christians in our own time. Both are the result of a drift away from the biblical idea of a muscular faith that expresses itself in all spheres of life and toward a dead and "religious" faith that is merely theological and ecclesiastical. Dietrich Bonhoeffer sought to awaken the church of his day to action, but as we know, they did not heed God's voice through him and invited the judgment they couldn't have dreamt would come. So the question for us now is whether we in the American church will heed the prophetic warnings of Bonhoeffer for our own time and avert the unfathomable horrors of our own silence and inaction.

Near the end of World War II, an imprisoned Bonhoeffer was ruminating about why the German church had failed, and suggested that they had needed a bold and "religionless Christianity"—but had instead opted for mere "religion." That is at the heart of what we will discuss: whether we might rise to that kind of faith and thereby avert the judgment Germany did not. In this book, I ultimately mean to sketch a vision of hope, that if we are now willing to pay the price God asks us to pay, we might not only avert or delay the coming judgment, but might launch a new era in history.

Among the reasons I have hope is that I am convinced God called me to write *Letter to the American Church*—and not merely to warn us of what lies ahead if we continue to fail to obey Him, but actually to call us to repent, which is His will for us. There is therefore a positive message at the heart of this book, just as there is a positive message at the heart of every one of God's warnings. We do not serve a peevish and fatalistic God who enjoins us to do His will merely so that He can say, "I told you so."

I am also hopeful because the response to *Letter to the American Church* has been extraordinarily positive. Many in the American church are clearly eager to repent of their failings and to find churches that understand where we are; they wish to be in the fight to which God now calls us. Countless people have written saying they have personally given scores of copies of the book to pastors, and several large conferences have been held to put the book's message in front of further hundreds of pastors. Finally, my preaching on the book at Pastor Rob McCoy's church in California led two Hollywood veterans in the congregation to make an extraordinary documentary film of the book, greatly multiplying the reach of this most urgent message.

Another reason that I am hopeful is rooted in Romans 8:28: "And we know that for those who love God all things work together for good, for those who are called according to His purpose." Is it not possible that God has allowed us to see how quickly evil can overtake us in these last four years precisely to wake up those who might still be awakened? Are the evils that we see on every front not perhaps God's tender mercies to us, just as a parent's chastisement of a child is ultimately in the hope that that child will change his behavior in the right direction and thereby avert the far greater chastisements to come if he does not?

It is a fact that because of the evils all around, many in our nation are finally waking up and seeing the evilness of evil—and realizing that they must shake off their inertia and take action. Many who would not even have used the term "evil" now see there is no other way to frame the things we are seeing, which seem to make no human or otherwise natural sense—and if one sees real evil and knows it to be evil, one is likely to turn to God.

Many across our country are waking up to see that freedom is not free, and that they must become involved in their communities, whether politically or otherwise. Many see that we have come to this awful pass precisely because we have not been living out our faith heroically and in every sphere. Therefore, this endless litany of evils that have befallen us—the nightmare of transgender madness, critical race theory, cultural Marxism, and the increasing corruption in all of our institutions, from increasingly authoritarian government to the propagandistic journalistic establishment and the complicity and groupthink of corporate America and beyond—need not be God's final and inevitable judgment. If we take action now, all of these things that have happened can be seen as God's merciful wake-up call to a slumbering church, specifically so that we might repent and do all in our power to live for God in a new way.

So we must wonder whether the present difficulties might indeed lead us toward something like a Second Reformation, one of which we have hardly dreamt. Martin Luther, in standing against the corruptions of his day, could not foresee the Reformation that would follow, but it was dramatically more far-reaching than mere church reformation, with ramifications throughout Europe that ultimately led to the ideas enshrined in the American Founding.

Who Was Dietrich Bonhoeffer?

For any unfamiliar with Dietrich Bonhoeffer's story, we may say that he was a German pastor and theologian who heroically opposed Adolf Hitler and the Nazis, and attempted to wake up the German church to stand strongly against them. I write about him at length in my 2010 biography, *Bonhoeffer: Pastor, Martyr, Prophet, Spy*. When Bonhoeffer saw the church fail in its duty to God and the German people, he eventually went outside the church and became involved in the assassination plots against Hitler, as we shall see. He became engaged to be married in 1942 and was imprisoned in 1943, where he continued to write. He was murdered by the Nazis in 1945, three weeks before the end of the war. He was thirty-nine years old.

Bonhoeffer was a theological genius, as well as a man of profound Christian faith. Perhaps what sets him apart most of all is that he knew that the goal of Christian faith was not merely to have good theology but actually to live out one's faith. He also knew that pretending faith is a merely "religious" exercise, or an exercise of intellectual theology, is not only a mistake, but an offense against God. Jesus did not come to Earth so that people would become theologians, attend church once a week, and hold to some doctrines. Bonhoeffer knew that God demanded everything of us, and when one doesn't live out one's faith, it only proves that one had no faith to begin with.

Finally, as we will say at the end of this book, we need to think of Bonhoeffer's use of the phrase "religionless Christianity" not merely as a lament for what might have been, but perhaps as a promise to us today of an extraordinarily hopeful way forward in which we really might live out our faith in a way unprecedented in human history.

CHAPTER ONE

Are We in the Last Days?

W e seem to be approaching the end of time.

Let that be the first sentence in the first chapter of this book, because this concept can be an infuriating trigger for those of us tempted toward mere "religion" and away from the full-throated "religionless Christianity" that we are putting forward in these pages. In a later chapter, we will deal with the evidence for the idea that we are indeed approaching the end of time. Because if we mean it seriously—and we do—it is not merely a dramatic statement, but one that requires our most profoundly serious attention. How could it not? To the extent that it is true, it is a uniquely powerful impetus for us to utterly reject whatever mere "religion" we have been substituting for the real thing, so that we might boldly live out a truly "religionless Christianity" with everything we have in us.

But before we deal with the evidence that we are indeed in the Last Days, let's in this first chapter confront the offensiveness of the concept. Our offense offers a clue to what's behind the "religious" thinking we are discussing and should help us see how we have fallen prey to this kind of merely "religious" thinking in many other things as well.

One of the core points about "religion" in the way we are using the term is that it does not oppose the God of the Bible openly in the way that atheism or paganism do. On the contrary, the thing we are calling mere "religion" always aims to give the appearance of following God. But it is actually a counterfeit.

From God's point of view, this is an abomination worse than open rebellion against Him. By way of example, the New Testament does not record Jesus thundering at the pervasive Hellenistic philosophies or paganism of His day, but it does record Him very often confronting those who publicly and sometimes ostentatiously claimed to represent the God of the Bible. It was these "religious" figures whom Jesus pointedly vilified not only as being far from the God they dared to represent, but as actually being His enemies (which we know they were). So we must confront the idea that it was the most "religious" figures of Jesus's day—those who revered the Old Testament and purported to worship its God more faithfully than anyone—who conspired to murder the very One sent by that God. So, "religion" in God's name—but actually divorced from God—is a satanic counterfeit.

The merely "religious" Christianity that we are discussing in this book always purports to represent the God of the Bible and His purposes. It always gives "good" and "religious" and "reasonable" reasons for the nonetheless false and wicked ideas it puts forward. In our day, what could be more reasonable than to say that talking about the End Times is an embarrassment to the faith, that it often pushes people away from taking God and the Bible seriously—and that it might even therefore endanger their very souls? There is, of course, much truth in that. What could be more reasonable than to express being fatigued by preachers carping about where we are on the "prophetic time clock"? Those obsessed with that really do often seem to forget that we are supposed to be living out our faith in the here and now, and not simply counting the seconds till the Last Trump. The people guilty of this are much like those who can only talk about demon possession and seem to think that anyone with a common cold must have it "cast out" rather than dealt with via the less dramatic solution of bed rest and chicken soup. There is much truth in seeing things this way, so it is all very understandable to a point.

But at what point does this kind of thinking push us into the opposite error? At what point are we straining out a gnat to swallow a camel? At what point are we pointing our finger at something that is not the principal issue, but a distraction from the principal issue?

When does the person who sees things "reasonably" fall into the opposite temptation of essentially behaving as though we will never actually be in the Last Days? And doesn't the person annoyed at those who see a demon behind every bush potentially fall into the error of behaving as though there are actually no such things as demons anymore, and as though Jesus does not tell us we have the power—and the obligation as the Church—to cast them out as He did? Isn't the temptation toward this kind of "reasonable" faith really our capitulation to secularism and to the idea that our faith really ought to be tame and reasonable and inoffensive, such that it can be kept in a safe corner away from the rest of the world? Don't we know many churches and church leaders who pretend there is never any reason for us to deal with the demonic as a reality or with the idea of Jesus's imminent return? Isn't that mostly secular approach to things—which we are calling dead "religion"—really the far more pressing problem for the American church today?

In our fear of seeming odd and off-putting to nonbelievers, haven't we accepted too much of the world's secular assessment of things? Has our salt lost its saltiness? How much of the secular cultural narrative have we accepted without realizing it, such that we are no longer the prophetic voices of God in our generation and are therefore a mere shadow of the true Christian faith? For what we imagine is the sake of our "witness," have we become the domesticated house cat version of what God intended to be a wild and fearsome lion of true faith? To what secular pressures and narratives have Christian leaders acceded, thinking it will help them reach the unchurched? Has it been an effective tack?

Bonhoeffer knew that the congregations in Germany that were merely "playing church" and not *being* the Church were precisely the reason the Nazis were able to take over. And it is those American churches doing the same thing that have opened the door to evil in our own time.

There are many ways in which Christians can be "religious" in this way. But when we think of the pastors of such churches, can we avoid thinking of Jesus vilifying the religious leaders of His own day as blind guides leading the blind? How nice it would be if it were a mere ditch in the Bruegel painting to which our leaders were leading their sleepwalking flocks and the culture around them, rather than an infinitely more nightmarish and consequential bottomless abyss!

As we will explain further, "religion" in this negative sense is any attempt to deal with the reality of this world—and, in particular, with the satanic evil in our world—in a way that believes it can cleverly avoid God's way of dealing with it. We believe that we may have a better, more sophisticated, and perhaps more *modern* way of dealing with it than God does. So we essentially set ourselves up as gods by inventing a "religious" system that avoids the more primitive or embarrassing ways of dealing with it. We will talk about the various ways that these counterfeit "religious" solutions manifest themselves in the chapters ahead.

For now, we can say that one signal way in which this "religious" instinct manifests itself is in softening those things that rub us the wrong way. Perhaps we wish to make the satanic evil that God defeated on the Cross somehow less evil—or better yet, not evil at all. Do we need to use those kinds of words and terms? We wish to soften the harsh reality of it all somehow and make the real problem at the heart of this world and human existence sound somehow less apocalyptic. And if we can do that, we can make the solution to that reduced problem much less dramatic and much more palatable than God's ghastly solution—which of course begins with the gruesome torture and death of Jesus on the Cross and continues with us moving forward in that reality of what was required to rescue us from the devil and Hell and death. Those two things mean we are in an inescapable, all-out war between the forces of light and darkness.

Wouldn't our lives be much less difficult and embarrassing if all that God required of us was to attend a church on Sundays and intellectually assent to some theological ideas while essentially living as the rest of the world lives? Why not avoid the apocalyptic language of being in a battle between God and the devil? That is precisely what "religion" masquerading as Christianity offers to us and what many who think themselves Christians have accepted as the Christian faith. But it is not the Christian faith. Indeed, it is a demonic religious parody of the Christian faith which the devil himself is always encouraging and which we must recognize and condemn—and repent of and flee from.

The difference between these two things is the difference between what Bonhoeffer in *The Cost of Discipleship* calls "cheap grace" and "costly grace." In a way, that is putting it quite mildly, because the difference between these two things is all the difference in the world. It really is the difference between Heaven and Hell. But how many Christians today are attending churches that are unwittingly guilty of precisely this error which Bonhoeffer so clearly pointed out, and which he—and now we too—can see as being the reason that satanic evil prevailed in his time? That is the nightmare horror of mere "religion."

There has always been an instinct in the church to excise what might make us uncomfortable or which might be unnecessarily off-putting to someone outside the fold. Sometimes this is genuinely helpful and a good thing, but more often than not—and certainly in Bonhoeffer's time and ours—it is the opposite. And when it is not helpful and good, it is "religion" masquerading as real faith.

So the idea that time will have an actual end—and that we might be drawing near to that ultimate finality—is sure to be near the top of any such list of uncomfortable things. This is why many Christians feel the need to keep this embarrassing idea at bay. They have already established in their minds that even if time will end, then surely that end must happen in some impossibly distant future. To suggest anything else is to be needlessly dramatic. "Respectable" Christians don't want to be associated with those embarrassing figures who proclaim "the end is nigh," only to blanch with embarrassment when they see it was not as nigh as they had insisted. Respectable Christians don't want to be associated with those embarrassing figures who say God speaks to them and can do miracles in our time just as He has always done.

If we relegate the end of time to some impossibly distant horizon, we don't need to be concerned with it any more than we need to be concerned with the projected end of the physical universe, which scientists affirm will happen many billions of years from now. What does it matter?

In Woody Allen's autobiographical film *Radio Days*, the character portraying him as a child wonders why he should bother doing his homework if the universe is eventually going to be destroyed, as his teachers say. What's the point of doing anything? This is perfectly logical if one doesn't believe in the God of the Bible. Only God gives real meaning to our lives; without Him, it is all meaninglessness and bleakness. To Allen's credit, he sees the truth of this, and has said so not only in his films but in many interviews. He has never seen the idea of a universe without God as anything other than logically absurd and inestimably bleak, which makes living here genuinely difficult, if we think about it. Of course, most people don't think about it, or they somehow push the question to the side.

But if God actually created the universe—and came to Earth, was crucified and resurrected, ascended into Heaven, and promised to return to bring final judgment, as all Christians purport to believe—our lives are filled not only with deep meaning but with tremendous urgency and purpose. But how many Christians have made their peace with a less dramatic view of things? How many of us have adopted a "religious" view that has sucked the vitality out of our faith and rendered us essentially secularist in our outlook?

It may not make sense to worry about the destruction of the earth or the physical universe billions of years from now (which is why Woody Allen's character's anxiety over it comes across as inspired comedy), but for avowed Christians to reject the clear biblical idea that we are living in the Last Days and that time really will end at some clear point—perhaps in the near future—is to reject the entire biblical view of time and history. Even to push it away as something in the distant future is essentially to reject it as a central aspect of our faith.

Why would we object to the idea that we might be approaching the end of time? What sort of faith do we have, exactly—and what are the boundaries of that faith? At what point do we simply say "enough" to people talking about the end of time? And by what right do we say it? Are we putting boundaries on our faith that God never created? Do we have a "religious" and "reasonable" view of the faith that has actually pushed God out without our realizing it?

As we have said, Christians are always tempted to shave away some part of the historical faith and find a more palatable substitute. If possible, we long for a faith that is more respectable—less wild and dramatic. We don't want to live like the early Christians who were martyred for their faith. We feel we live in a more sophisticated time and simply don't need to be as dramatic as they were. We can have our safe, acceptable, and respectable Christianity, and we do not need to engage in this war between good and evil as others in the past have done. We want to keep our faith within certain boundaries. We don't want to embarrass ourselves in front of our secular neighbors. We simply want to go to church and otherwise conduct our lives as sophisticated secular people. We don't want secular people to think of us as odd, because won't that push them away from potentially accepting our faith when the time is right? Aren't our concerns really about evangelism? (This is part of what I called "the idol of evangelism" in my book *Letter to the American Church*.)

But what if we are actually living in a time when this is a fatal error of judgment? What if we have actually believed a satanic lie? What if we are living in a time when it is incredibly important that we see the need to put away our fussy "religious" objections and turn to face the reality that God Himself longs for us to accept and face?

What evils must befall us before we wake up and live out the faith we claim to have? Why do we think we are somehow immune from becoming tools of Satan in exactly the same way as so many otherwise good Christians in Nazi Germany?

When Christians Adopt a Secular View

One particular way we have drifted to our current place has been by turning the stark historical events of the Bible into mere stories or mythical events. To be clear, the great moments of God's story with mankind do partake of the mythical because they are epochal events in which God and eternity enter time and space. So in that sense of the word, all the events of Scripture are mythical. But we must be supremely clear that they are also *actual events in time and history*. And this matters infinitely. We cannot relegate them to the merely mythical, as though they happened "once upon a time"—which is to say that they never actually happened at all. This is one of the ways that our "religious" instinct often deals with the parts we don't like. It puts "religious" reality in a separate box from the rest of reality, as though our faith has no bearing on the rest of reality when, of course, the exact opposite is true. If our faith exists apart from the rest of reality, then it is meaningless.

This is precisely what dead "religion" always does. It drains the actual and infinitely powerful meaning from faith and turns it into something like a hobby. We do it in our basement when we have free time. It doesn't bother anyone outside our basement. But real faith in the God of the Bible is exactly the opposite of this. It spreads into the real world in every dimension, because faith in the God of the Bible is faith in the One who called Himself Truth and who created every part of the reality in which we live. Faith in that God cannot be contained by any means. If you have been a party to any church that is guilty of this, you must yourself repent, probably by leaving that church. Do you dare to do that?

Will the Lord forgive you if you don't?

Have you or your church become so secularized that you have believed the lie that your faith should be kept in a religious corner where it doesn't bother anyone? Keep in mind that that view of the Christian faith is the one that prevails in the Communist Party in China today, where you may do as you like in a certain, officially sanctioned building on a Sunday morning—but when you leave that building, you must bow to the secular authority of the state. Keep in mind that that view of the Christian faith is the one shared by Adolf Hitler, which we will see clearly in chapter five. And keep in mind that this is the view of the Church held by Satan himself; he only needs to keep us in our religious corner in order to impose his will on the world. With the Church in that corner, the rest of the field belongs to him. Will you and your church remain as you are and thereby be guilty of complicity in Satan's will for the world—or will you wake up, repent, and participate in God's will for the world?

The reason we are where we are now in America is because the American church has voluntarily adopted this secular—and ultimately satanic view—of the Church. We have bought the lie that the only reality with which we need to concern ourselves is the "theological" part, as though it were an island unconnected to the rest of reality. This is the central lie of our time, and it is precisely this false view that marks the fatal secularization of the Church unto death.

Bonhoeffer could see that this view was leading Germany down a path of something unimaginably horrible. He tried to awaken the German church to this fact, but of course we know that they slumbered on. When Bonhoeffer wrote the words "religionless

Christianity" to a friend in 1944, he was creating a term to describe the real thing—the true, vibrant, fearless Christian faith—that would have enabled Germany to avoid the unthinkable nightmare of what by that time had already happened. In the same prison letters, he said that the "religion" of the German church had in fact pushed Christ out. Theirs was not "religionless Christianity" but a "Christless religion." He knew that either we repent of these safe and "religious" efforts, or we cease to be the Church. At some point, God runs out of patience with those churches that have ceased to be His Church. Just as Jesus cursed the fig tree, He will curse those churches that fail to bear the real fruit they were planted to bear. God is a judge, and His justice will not wait forever.

Perhaps we have not ourselves experienced miracles or seen people miraculously healed. We have not seen God part the Red Sea or do anything historically dramatic in that way. We tell ourselves that perhaps He once did, but He no longer does so. And even if we do see terrible things happening around us, we are not inclined to see them as signs of the End Times. We are instead inclined to blithely wave them away as anomalies and declare that "the pendulum swings back and forth." We tell ourselves that, at present, we are only experiencing one of those pendulum swings, and of course, the pendulum will swing back again. Any talk of our going past a point of no return—of going over a cliff or falling into an abyss or coming to the end of time—sounds like unnecessary drama. There is no sense in taking to the barricades as though we were in some kind of war.

But what if we are wrong? The German Christians of Bonhoeffer's time were wrong in precisely this way and gave precisely the same excuses for their inaction that many Christians are giving today. That alone should get our serious attention. They may not have come to the boundary of human history, but the scores of millions who were murdered or otherwise had their lives destroyed might wonder what the difference was.

God acts in history. That is the biblical view. At a certain point, He created the universe—and space and time. At a certain moment, He called Abraham out of Ur of the Chaldees and spoke to him about his future and the future of the world, which would come through the people that God would bring into being from Abraham's child, Isaac. These are not mere myths and stories.

Moses at a certain point spoke with God and came to lead God's people out of Egypt and slavery. We accept that God miraculously parted the Red Sea so that the Israelites would see God's power on their behalf and never forget it. And of course, at a certain point in human history, God sent His own Son into this world, into time and space. This did not happen "once upon a time," but in actual history—at a particular time and in a particular place, every bit as particular as the murder of Abraham Lincoln on a Friday in April 1865 in a theater in our nation's capital.

The God of the Bible has acted in history and will act again. He is acting this minute in myriad ways and performing miracles—although many church leaders will refuse to acknowledge this, having believed the heartbreaking doctrine of cessationism. We must have faith to believe that God is not asleep but is alive and awake, and that He is now calling His Church to come to life too and participate with Him in His will for this country and the world.

Let him who has ears to hear listen: this is the hour of the American church.

CHAPTER TWO

Bonhoeffer's Diagnosis

From his Berlin prison cell in 1944, Dietrich Bonhoeffer wrote a letter to his closest friend Eberhard Bethge. Bonhoeffer was ruminating on how the German church had failed to stand against the evil of the Nazis, and in doing so coined the term "religionless Christianity." He was writing in a way that he obviously never intended for any eyes other than those of his closest friend, who was deeply familiar with Bonhoeffer's theological thinking. Bethge could understand Bonhoeffer's cryptic shorthand version of what he would have said very differently if it had been written for public consumption. Bonhoeffer wrote many letters to Bethge during this period, hoping that he might preserve them as fodder for a book he would write in the future. To that end, Bethge actually put these letters in a gas mask canister and buried them in the backyard of Bonhoeffer's parents' home in Berlin.

After Bonhoeffer was executed by the Nazis in 1945, Bethge felt it might be a good idea to let the world see these letters. So a few years later, he released them in a volume titled *Letters and Papers from Prison*. The problem was that many who first encountered Bonhoeffer in these letters—and who obviously did not understand his deep and abiding theologically orthodox faith—tended to interpret them along their own theologically liberal lines. So for many decades, much of what he wrote—especially his use of the phrase "religionless Christianity"—was utterly misunderstood. Many earnestly believed that in the last two years of his life, Bonhoeffer had skittered away from a genuine biblical faith into some kind of agnostic ethical humanism. Nothing could have been further from the truth, but this tragic and preposterous misreading of what Bonhoeffer believed was pushed into the world for many decades.

The fact is that Bonhoeffer's theology—and his essential diagnosis of the state of the German church—did not change at all toward the end of his life. On the contrary, it was amazingly consistent throughout his adult life. Indeed, the central ideas that we may sum up in his phrase "religionless Christianity" were present in some of his earliest thinking. In fact, when Bonhoeffer was just twenty-two—sixteen years before he coined the famous phrase—he gave a series of three lectures to high school students in Spain in which he laid out most of the ideas that he would expand upon over the years, culminating in his use of the phrase "religionless Christianity" the year before his death.

At that time, Bonhoeffer was serving for one year as the associate pastor of a German-speaking parish in Barcelona, and it was in these lectures to high school students that we first see him clearly diagnosing the failure of the German church. In a word, he said the process of secularization—inside and outside the church—was the central issue. He had no idea at that time how dramatically and quickly the Nazis would exploit this secularization process in a few years, and to what horrific ends. But in order for the Nazis to silence the churches and thereby take over Germany, the slow secularization of German culture was centrally important, as Bonhoeffer would see soon enough.

Bonhoeffer was born in 1906. By age thirteen, he knew he wished to study theology, and as soon as he was old enough, he did so. From 1924 until 1927, he had a front-row seat at Berlin University, studying under the famous Adolf von Harnack, who had himself been a disciple of the legendary Friedrich Schleiermacher. Although Bonhoeffer admired these men's scholarship, he differed with them theologically, since they were essentially liberal proponents of the very kind of scholarship that led to the problems Bonhoeffer would soon be diagnosing and speaking out about until the end of his life. Bonhoeffer received his doctorate at the remarkable age of twenty-one, and the legendary theologian Karl Barth pronounced his dissertation "a theological miracle."

In 1928—a year after getting his doctorate and five years before Hitler took the reins of power in Germany—Bonhoeffer found himself helping Spanish teenagers understand the true and vital nature of the Christian faith, and spoke to them about the secularization that had been taking place in Germany for many decades.

It is remarkable to think that this young man had thought these things out long before he became the Bonhoeffer we now know, who stood so heroically against the Nazis. It is also remarkable that someone who could write at the highest theological level could communicate the faith so effectively to laypeople—and to young people, too. This gets to the heart of Bonhoeffer's theology: that one must not only have the right theology, but must be able to communicate it to common people living out their nontheological lives—and that one must live out one's faith, else it is all a sham. From the beginning, he understood that faith must not be mere ideas, but must enter one's real life in all aspects. It must be lived out.

It was in the second of these lectures that Bonhoeffer spoke of the secularization of the church. It is remarkable that he didn't talk down to these young people or soften the difficult things he was saying. He respected these teenagers enough to make several dramatic statements, many of which likely would have shocked the parents in the congregation.

First of all, Bonhoeffer put forth the very sobering idea that most Christians had exiled Christ from their lives. What in the world could that mean? But it lay at the heart of what he would say in the years ahead. It was the opposite of what he would later call "religionless Christianity"; it was actually what we might call "Christless religion." It is what some today have called mere "church-ianity" and bespeaks an expression of faith that has drifted away from the radicalness of genuine Christianity. It is a watered-down faith that has made its peace with secular society—and with evil, too.

"Of course we build Him a temple," Bonhoeffer said in his lecture, "but we live in our own houses."[1] He said that we had exiled Christ to a place "into which one gladly withdraws for a couple of hours, but only to get back to one's place of work immediately afterward."[2]

This is the core of Bonhoeffer's views on dead "religion." We create a safe and truncated version of the real thing—but of course we pretend it's the real thing. It was a sobering accusation for a twenty-two-year-old associate pastor to make. He went on to say that we cannot give Jesus just "a small compartment of our spiritual life."[3]

"The religion of Christ is not a tidbit after one's bread," he said. "On the contrary, it is the bread or it is nothing. People should at least understand and concede this if they call themselves Christian."[4]

Bonhoeffer already had his finger on the very pulse of the situation, and he would spend the rest of his life explicating what he said that day. That's because the error he was pointing out without dramatic urgency in 1928 would become increasingly pronounced and exponentially more harmful when the Nazis began to exploit it for their evil ends.

In his lecture, Bonhoeffer then turned to another aspect of dead "religion." In words that will bring to mind C. S. Lewis—who, though eight years older than Bonhoeffer, was not yet a Christian in 1928—Bonhoeffer continued:

> One admires Christ according to authentic categories as an aesthetic genius, calls him the greatest ethicist, one admires his going to his death as a heroic sacrifice for his ideas. Only one thing one doesn't do: one doesn't take him seriously. That is, one doesn't bring the center of his or her own life into contact with the claim of Christ to speak the revelation of God and to be that revelation.
>
> One maintains a distance between himself or herself and the word of Christ, and allows no serious encounter to take place. I can doubtless live with or without Jesus as a religious genius, as an ethicist, as a gentleman—just as, after all, I can also live without Plato and Kant.... Should, however, there be something in Christ that claims my life entirely with the full seriousness that here God himself speaks and if the world of God once became present only in Christ, then Christ has not only relative but absolute, urgent significance for me.... Understanding Christ means taking Christ seriously. Understanding this claim means taking seriously his absolute claim on our commitment.

And it is now of importance for us to clarify the seriousness
of this matter and to extricate Christ from the secularization
process in which he has been incorporated since the
Enlightenment.[5]

At last, we hear him refer to the "secularization process," which
was at the dead center of how the Christian faith—both in his time
and in our own—has been bled white, so that it is no longer the true
and vibrant faith for which so many martyrs died but has instead
become a withered and desiccated imposter.

Bonhoeffer made another important point during this lecture
which equally helps us diagnose "religionless Christianity": If the
Christian faith is simply assenting to the ethics of Jesus, then it is not
the Christian faith at all but mere moralism and mere "religion." So
it is not different from many other religions in this aspect, which
implies that we may just as well ignore it.

"Factually speaking," Bonhoeffer said, "Christ has given scarcely
any ethical prescriptions that were not to be found already with the
contemporary Jewish rabbis or in pagan literature."[6] Bonhoeffer was
not pulling any punches. He makes it clear that Jesus did not come to
this planet to exhort us to be moral, as important as that might be.
At the center of His mission was the idea that if we tried of our own
accord to be moral—to climb the ladder to Heaven in our own
strength—we were not only missing the point of Jesus's message, but
working against it. We were being "religious" and not genuine
Christians. Far worse, we were involved in what must ultimately be
deemed a satanic usurpation of God's role.

Bonhoeffer already saw this in 1928, but even he could have no
inkling of what the near future held for the German church and the
spiritual war that would break out into the open with the most

nightmarish results. He returned to Germany in 1929 and continued to teach and preach along these lines. But because he was still a year too young to be ordained, he chose to come to America in 1930, spending a year in New York City at Union Theological Seminary.

No one could have predicted it, but that year in America would change him the most dramatically. For one thing, he saw that the Protestant American churches were very similar to those in Germany. Their theological liberalism had pulled them away from a full-throated expression of biblical Christianity, and as in Germany, they had essentially become secularized. Union Theological Seminary was especially guilty of this, much to Bonhoeffer's chagrin. But there was one place in America where he did see real faith being lived out: in what he called "the negro churches."

Bonhoeffer had befriended a black fellow Union student from Alabama named Frank Fisher, who invited him to visit Abyssinian Baptist Church in Harlem, which was then the largest church in the country. Bonhoeffer was astonished at what he saw. The congregants had not adopted the liberal theology of the socially respectable white churches in New York, and their faith therefore went far beyond mere theology and religiosity. So they did not shrink from speaking out politically on issues that seemed important. For example, they were especially vocal about the lynchings happening at that time in the South. And their musical worship was transporting to Bonhoeffer. It was far more visceral than the buttoned-up hymns he had grown up with. It was all quite unlike anything he had ever experienced.

When Bonhoeffer returned to Germany in 1931, his friends perceived a difference in him. His faith had somehow been deepened. He had seen what real Christian faith could look like, and he was determined somehow to bring it to Germany. And what could be a better time to do so? Because just as he returned, the Nazis were dramatically on the rise. Bonhoeffer could see that now the real test of the German church would come. Could they be made to see the desperate need to kick away their mere "religion" and really be the Church, as God intended? Would they be willing to see that it was their job to speak against what the Nazis were offering?

So Bonhoeffer preached and taught along these lines at every opportunity. But as we know, his exhortations fell on mostly deaf ears. Hitler officially took power in Germany in 1933, and it was not very long afterward that Bonhoeffer realized the German church simply was not up to what God required of them. Where there might have been real faith, there was mostly mere "religion." It was deeply frustrating. He saw that the secularization process had so weakened the church over the decades that now, when it mattered most, they balked from taking the decisive and selfless action that God willed for them to take.

Bonhoeffer continued to fight as he could, valiantly trying to awaken the German church to its calling to be the "conscience of the state," as he put it. He was central in the creation of the Confessing Church, which refused to bow to the Nazis. Nonetheless, by 1935 the battle was essentially over. The church's hesitation and inaction had given Hitler every opportunity to silence it, which he did. Still, Bonhoeffer did not give up, but fought on in other ways, as we shall see.

In 1936 he wrote what became his most famous book, *The Cost of Discipleship*. In it, he again diagnosed the church's secularization over time as the central issue. "As Christianity spread," he wrote, "the Church became more secularized."[7] And so "the costliness of grace gradually faded." He wrote that the "world was Christianized, and grace became its common property."[8] In other words, in the fourth century—after Constantine made Christianity the official religion of the Roman Empire—everyone became "officially" Christian. As a result, almost no one was actually Christian in the way they had been under persecution. The bar to becoming a Christian had been lowered, and many people over the centuries lost the fire of those who had had to fight for their faith. Bonhoeffer continued:

> Yet the Church of Rome did not altogether lose the earlier vision. It is highly significant that the Church was astute enough to find room for the monastic movement.... Here on the outer fringe of the Church was a place where the older vision was kept alive. Here men still remember that grace costs, that grace means following Christ. Here they left all they had for Christ's sake, and endeavored daily to practice his rigorous commands. Thus monasticism became a living protest against the secularization of Christianity and the cheapening of grace. But the church was wise enough to tolerate this protest, and to prevent it from developing to its logical conclusion. It thus succeeded in relativizing it, even using it in order to justify the secularization of its own life.[9]

In other words, there were still some within the Church over the centuries for whom Christ really was everything. But these were now only those Christians who took holy orders and had separated from the world. The rest of Christendom was essentially secularized. So going through the religious motions of attending church—and performing various other rituals—seemed to be all that was necessary.

So now in *The Cost of Discipleship*—as Hitler was remaking Germany and the German church in his own image—Bonhoeffer was explaining how it had all happened and laying out what it means to be an actual Christian: to give one's all in living out the faith. The lie that our faith is something we keep in a compartment will not work. Either we live it out fully and understand that God demands that of us, or we will see we are not only failing to do what God wants, but are actually working with His enemies against Him.

When church leaders thought it prudent to keep the faith in a religious box—so that they and their congregants would not threaten either the surrounding secular culture or the secular state—they had already seen to it that the church was not the Church. At some point, these Christian leaders would wake up to what they had allowed to happen and would see their complicity in trading real "religionless Christianity" for mere religion. But by then, it would be too late.

Nowhere do we see this more clearly than in the sobering story of Bonhoeffer's friend Martin Niemöller, which we will tell in chapter five.

CHAPTER THREE

What Is Religion?

Now the serpent was more crafty than any other beast
of the field that the Lord God had made. He said to the
woman, "Did God actually say, 'You shall not eat of any
tree in the garden'?"And the woman said to the serpent,
"We may eat of the fruit of the trees in the garden, but
God said, 'You shall not eat of the fruit of the tree that
is in the midst of the garden, neither shall you touch it,
lest you die.'" But the serpent said to the woman, "You
will not surely die. For God knows that when you eat
of it your eyes will be opened, and you will be like God,
knowing good and evil."

—Genesis 3:1–5

To talk about "religionless Christianity" as God's answer to evil, we must first explain more fully what we mean by "religion" in the negative sense in which Bonhoeffer and others have used it. The simplest answer to what religion is in this negative sense becomes clear when we say what religion is in the more normal, general sense: religion is humanity's attempt to solve our most fundamental problems.

Since the dawn of our race, human beings have always known that something was deeply wrong. Life was always difficult, to put it mildly. People suffered and died. Crops often failed, or game was scarce and people starved. So every culture created "religious" ways to deal with these problems. There are no exceptions to this. It lies at the heart of the human condition in all times and places, stretching back as far as anyone can trace. This is the history of "religion," and it is the story of mankind.

It is especially curious that every culture throughout the eons somehow believed that we were guilty of something, and that in order to have any hope of remedying our problems, we somehow had to deal with our guilt. So in various ways, we attempted to appease the "gods" whom we thought had control over our lives—the ones whom we believed had reckoned us as guilty and were therefore punishing us.

In our varied religious rituals, we sacrificed animals and often human beings to appease these gods; somehow intuiting that their appeasement required actual lives and actual blood. We attempted to answer their demands in this way, pathetically hoping to move them to act on our behalf. This is the story of many of the pagan religions throughout world history and today (whereby human beings are actually attempting to appease demons whom they believe to be gods). It is like paying a powerful criminal to protect us from lesser criminals. In the end, we were always doing business with criminals and are always in their debt—and never genuinely free. Whatever we got from these demons or gods was worth less than what we paid them, and infinitely so. Nonetheless, we knew no better way of dealing with the problem and continued making our payments.

Other religious ways of dealing with this fundamental problem of the divide between us and those in the spiritual realm involve adhering to moral rules and behavior, as though our own moral and behavioral sacrifices were the answer. Martin Luther's attempts as a young monk to do this are a good example of this in a Christian context and illustrate its ultimate bankruptcy. But many cultures and religions have actually taught—and still teach—that it is possible for some human beings to bridge this divide entirely and somehow reach the godhead by becoming especially "holy," and that these enlightened human beings can provide our solutions.

The idea is always that doing certain things while refraining from doing other things might enable us to climb the ladder from this world into the next, from slavery in the material world into freedom in the realm of divinity. Many Eastern religions subscribe to this idea. But we must be clear from the outset that God's interventions with us throughout history have been to show us that we could never solve the problem in these ways, and that He Himself was the only One who could repair the breach between us and Him. God ultimately sent Jesus to end such moralism and "religion" forever.

But we know that many forms of the Jewish and Christian faiths nonetheless also have been guilty of missing God's solution and of devolving to mere religion. Instead of having real faith in the God of the Bible, they essentially substituted mere "religion" and "religiosity" so that they were using the outward forms of God's biblical solution but actually avoiding God and attempting to solve the problem themselves. The notoriously corrupt religious leaders of Jesus's time combined blood sacrifice with moral behavior in an admixture that repulsed Jesus and which He condemned openly as being precisely the opposite of what His Heavenly Father required. So it is important to say again that purporting to worship the God of the Bible does not necessarily mean we are actually doing so. Jews before Jesus and Christians after Jesus have often been guilty of practicing "mere religion." That is the principal point we are discussing in this book.

But before we move to the idea that Jews in Jesus's day and
Christians ever since have often corrupted God's idea of faith in Him
and turned to mere "religion," it's important to underscore the fact
that when the God of the Bible enters the picture of human history,
His divine plan is indeed to end religion once and for all. This is why,
when those who purport to worship Him indulge in mere "religion,"
it is especially horrific.

The story of the Bible is the story of God reaching out to us in
order to end the "religion" ubiquitous in human cultures. It is the
story of God creating a people for Himself and of finally providing
the sacrifice that no mere "religion" could provide. God unequivocally
puts Himself forth as the only solution to our problems. We can never
hope to appease Him sufficiently via blood sacrifices, nor climb the
moral and behavioral ladder from where we are to where He is in
Heaven. He wants us to see that the gulf between us is infinite and
we are powerless to bridge it. Our guilt is not only real, but infinite—so
our most generous blood sacrifices and our best moral behavior can
never make up the infinite distance separating us from a holy God.

Only if we genuinely accept this assessment of our situation and face
this reality can God help us. He who is infinite and perfect and holy and
all-powerful and omniscient and omnipresent can solve the problem by
traversing the distance between Himself and us. He who is holy and
perfect and infinite can pay the infinite price of our guilt.

So every imaginable "religious" solution to the problem is our
attempt to solve it apart from God. But the only actual solution to the
problem is for us to understand that only God can solve it. The story
of "religion" is the story of our fall from grace and our attempt to find
grace without God—and then the story of God trying to help us see
that we cannot find grace apart from Him.

Religion as a Satanic Project

Before we continue, we should say that it is remarkable and a great mystery that even before mankind's Fall in Eden, we nonetheless were confronted with and believed the satanic and "religious" lie that we could become like God ourselves and that we could reach Heaven without Him. In Genesis 3, we read the story of how we listened to the lies of the serpent and were tragically receptive to the idea that we could dispense with God. And more than that: that we could do *better* than what God had given us. It is a conundrum, but Scripture recounts how we believed Satan's lie, took the forbidden fruit, and ate it. It is remarkable that even with no need whatever for any remedy—since we were in Paradise, in the presence of God, with no division between us and Him—we nonetheless somehow accepted the satanic lie that we might improve our situation if only we took things into our own hands.

So the idea behind "religion" as we are using it here is the idea of getting to Heaven our own way, not God's way. Of course, this is not only impossible but has at its heart the satanic idea of supplanting God. Satan said that God was our adversary and that He didn't wish us to eat the forbidden fruit because if we did so, we would "be as gods." Therefore, what we are calling "religion" in this negative sense is an unavoidably satanic project. It is the idea that we would become "gods," which is Satan's idea for himself. That is at the heart of all we are taking about.

But there is still more.

While in Eden—after we had eaten the fruit and saw that we were naked and were, for the first time, actually divorced from God because of our sin—we did not realize our mistake, turn to God for forgiveness, and ask Him to help us. Somehow even then, our pride and foolishness mandated that we deal with the problem ourselves.

So Adam and Eve—now suddenly aware of their nakedness—endeavored to fix things by making aprons of fig leaves, as though that would sufficiently cover their nakedness and solve the problem they had created. We may regard the making of those fig-leaf aprons as the first truly "religious" act. They attempted to fool God and themselves into thinking that they had solved the problem. Of course, they had no idea of the magnitude of the problem they had created in their disobedience to God. They had no idea that there was not merely *some* distance between them and God, but that it was infinite, and therefore their capacities to breach that gap were insufficient. They had no idea that they could not traverse that distance, or that only God could do so. They had no idea that the evil and sin and sickness and death they had allowed to enter the world by their disobedience could only be defeated by God Himself, and that He would do so by coming to Earth as a human being and paying the ultimate price of death in our place.

And as we say, the story of God with mankind after Eden is the story of God preparing us for His ultimate answer to our degraded state. The Old Testament is the story of how God created a people for Himself and then intervened on their behalf over and over, loving them forward through His plan for them, despite their constant ingratitude and disobedience, and finally through them bringing into existence His Messiah to be the ultimate sacrifice for our sins. It is not a "religious" story, but rather the story of God ending religion forever.

But the subject of this book is that *despite* God having done this, we who purport to believe in Him and in His ultimate solution of salvation have often backslidden into merely "religious" attempts to solve our sin problem. Of course, we have seen human beings who do not claim to worship the God of the Bible make their own attempts to solve the problem, whether via paganism or some other religions, or via nakedly atheistic and secular efforts at utopia. But what both Bonhoeffer and we here are concerned with is when these "religious" efforts are made by the supposed people of God. Bonhoeffer saw it in the German church of the 1930s and realized it was not sufficient to stand against the satanic evil of the Nazi regime.

So when we talk about "religion" in his time and our own, we are talking about precisely this instinct to push God out of the way, usually without seeing that is what we are doing. We want to achieve heaven—or utopia or nirvana or whatever we might call it—on our own terms. We want to leap up into Heaven, but we do not want to do it by obeying God. And of course, the secret reason for this is that we really want to be God ourselves.

The idea of having to go through Jesus and the Cross and death on Good Friday in order to get to the part where we can emerge from the grave on Sunday is not our first choice. Who wants to die in order to live again if we can just evolve upward from our current life into a better life? We have believed the lie that that is possible. Satan gave us our first crack at it in the Garden of Eden, but this tendency and temptation lies within each of our sinful breasts at all times, even within the Church.

So if we can make our efforts along these lines seem "spiritual" and "Christian," we can pretend that we are doing something wonderful and "spiritual" that will benefit all. We don't want anyone to notice that it is ultimately selfish and ignoble, that we actually are attempting to clamber into Heaven and murder God and take His place. We don't want to see that in ourselves any more than the religious leaders of Jesus's day wanted to believe they were capable of murdering God in human form. But that is precisely what Satan wished to do then, and still wishes to do today and always. And he—like the White Witch in C. S. Lewis's *The Lion, the Witch, and the Wardrobe*—wants to trick us into thinking that we will be a part of his wonderful kingdom when we all get there together. But of course, once there, we will discover that we are not in Heaven but in Hell, and that rather than treating us as his coheirs in a wonderful kingdom, we will discover we are his slaves for eternity in the worst nightmare imaginable.

One final image we should put forth here in the outset of our discussion of "religion"—which, as we say, is the satanic project to solve our problems without God—is the story of the Tower of Babel from Genesis 11. We will come back to this later on, because it provides a genuinely fascinating image for where we are at this moment in human history and how, in our contemporary "religious" efforts, we are attempting to do something very similar to what the builders of the Tower of Babel were trying to do: achieve godhead for ourselves via human means.

To reprise the basics, we read in Genesis 11 that all mankind knew they had been exiled from Paradise and wanted to find their way back. So sometime after the Flood, they proposed to build a city with a tower so high that it would pierce into the very heavens. We imagine that it must have been a ziggurat structure (which is simply a stepped pyramid)—but if we think of the size of the Great Pyramid at Cheops in Giza made by the Egyptians nearly five thousand years ago, we have some idea of what was possible even in distant antiquity. (The Great Pyramid originally stood nearly five hundred feet high and was the tallest structure in the world for nearly four thousand years.) In any case, we know from Genesis that God confounded the efforts at Babel by causing everyone to speak different languages so that their attempt to reach Heaven was thwarted.

The story of that thwarted effort represents the first time that all of humankind attempted in a united way to reach godhead on our own—not merely without God, but in open defiance of Him. It is this utopian instinct that has arisen in less-united forms throughout history that we are calling "religion" and which is, at its roots, a satanic project.

More to the point, it is something we are doing now again on a united, global level in a way that we have not done since the Tower of Babel. This is an inescapably chilling thing to consider, and we will do so in a later chapter.

CHAPTER FOUR

Characteristics of Mere "Religion"

When we talk of mere "religion," we are talking about the efforts throughout history of those who call themselves Christians to reinvent the faith so that it is no longer the actual Christian faith, but some false version of it. The key to this entirely unholy project is to convince ourselves and others that we are not changing the Christian faith or getting rid of it, but rather that we are somehow refining it for the better. We wrongly imagine that we are making it better by underscoring its best and most essential elements and doing away with the superfluous elements that we believe obscure its true essence. In reality, the only thing we are doing to the faith is destroying it.

Before we talk about the various ways this evil has been done, we must aver that there have indeed been genuine and good attempts to reform the faith, most of which any sincere Christian would see as positive. Such attempts at reformation have taken place both before and after Martin Luther and the Protestant Reformation. Francis of Assisi and many others throughout the history of the Roman Catholic

Church saw that things had drifted away from God's intentions and sought to bring the Church back to its roots. Jan Hus, John Wycliffe, William Tyndale, Savonarola, and others made such efforts but were murdered for doing so by the religious "elites" who opposed them. To some extent, this is precisely the story of Jesus Himself—although His is a unique case in history and presents the ultimate picture of the war between "mere religion" and real faith.

But what we are talking about in this book is not these good efforts, but their opposites. We are talking about those efforts that only pretend to get at the "real thing" in the Christian faith. Most of these efforts attempt to carve away those legitimate and vital aspects of the faith that make some uncomfortable and aim to construct something else that purports to give us all the benefits of the faith without the parts we dislike. Sometimes these efforts have resulted in heretical sects, while others have simply undermined the Church from within, weakening it so that it is only a husk of the actual Church of Jesus Christ. This was the case with the German church in the early 1930s, as Bonhoeffer saw, and it is the case with much of the American church today.

As we have said, Bonhoeffer in 1928 explained in a lecture to teenagers that one of the principal examples of this phenomenon first occurred in the Christian faith roughly two hundred years earlier during the Enlightenment. He chalked it up to the forces of secularization which had, in his day, overwhelmed European society and infiltrated the church. Of course, in the years since Bonhoeffer spoke about them, those same forces have continued their destruction.

For example, many in the Enlightenment began touting "reason" over "faith," as though these two things were somehow at odds. So in order to keep what they liked in the Christian faith, the Enlightenment "rationalists" praised the ethics of Jesus but foreswore the miraculous elements of the gospels. Thomas Jefferson infamously dared to create a bowdlerized edition of the New Testament in which he sliced out all of its miracles and supernatural aspects. Without all of the embarrassing hocus-pocus of the supernatural, secularists created a "religion" of what they believed were Christian ethics. Of course, this quickly becomes an absurd project in which one loses not just the miracles but the ethics too. That's because without the God behind them, the ethics become utterly subjective and must ultimately vanish. Not only do the ethics vanish, but the process usually leads to the bloodbath "ethics" of the guillotine, as they did in the French Revolution.

Nonetheless, since the eighteenth century, many "sophisticated" people began shifting away from the God of the Bible—as though science and reason made belief in Him impossible—but for some reason continued to praise the ethics of Jesus, as though the real point of His appearance among us must have been to get us all to be morally better people. This is one way in which moralistic "religion" displaces actual Christian faith, and we have seen many versions of it in the centuries since it first appeared.

This general trend continued through the latter part of the nineteenth century, when German "higher criticism" believed that it was dismantling the core doctrines of the Bible, and another effort was made to see what kernels might still be saved. In the twentieth century, the "Modernists" and "Progressives" decided that all the embarrassing aspects of the "Fundamentalists" must be kicked away and replaced with social programs so that feeding the hungry and caring for the poor—again, the "ethics of Jesus"—were put front and center, while the need to believe in the miraculous elements of the gospels was set aside. Bonhoeffer saw this in full bloom at Union Seminary in New York when he arrived in 1930.

Our own man-made "religion" usually wishes to dispense with the uncomfortable—and perhaps embarrassing—aspects of the Christian faith. We prefer to have a nice, tidy faith, one that avoids discussions about talking snakes or floating arks or manna from Heaven, for example, and that perhaps gets us out of church at a reasonable hour on Sundays. But this is ultimately impossible—and it is a bargain with the devil. This must be a maddening conundrum for those who want the goodness of God without God Himself, because it can never be achieved. But human beings will continue to try to achieve it, because it is in our sinful nature to do so.

Twisting Christian Faith into Mere Religion

So what are some of the ways we end up subverting the Christian faith by trying to turn it into something more palatable? Truth can be twisted in a thousand different ways; let's consider some of them.

For example, one way in which this negative "religious" instinct has manifested itself is when people attempt to pull the great mysteries of God downward into something manageable. Jesus declared that He was "the Way, the Truth, and the Life," but it is our sinful instinct to make this more manageable. We might say, for example, if you assent to these doctrines, you are in the club. Sometimes we add a handful of activities. *Do these things and don't do these things.*

Perhaps you have heard someone say you only need to pray the so-called "Sinner's Prayer." Or maybe you filled out the comment card at church and said that you had accepted Jesus as your personal Lord and savior. But these abbreviated versions are bastardizations and counterfeits of the real faith. God wants us to live our whole lives in obedience to Him; the temptation to create these shortcuts is ultimately a "religious" enterprise.

Of course, if you really have accepted Jesus in this way, then various actions will follow. Things will change. There will be fruit, so to speak. But what if you claim to believe and yet there is no fruit? The Scripture says that "faith without works is dead." Here is a fly in the ointment: God is telling us that if we have really and truly given our lives to Him, we will live differently. We will want to please Him with every part of our lives. We will live in gratitude to Him for what He has made possible for us via His sacrifice on the Cross, and we really will want to be conformed to His image, to be like Him. We are meant not simply to become "saved," but to mature in our faith. We are to become disciples and to make disciples, not merely converts. To become "saved" is not to cross the finish line, but to cross the starting line.

What has been called the "seeker friendly" version of the Christian faith—which focuses almost exclusively on making converts and not disciples—is one modern example of "dead religion." It is sometimes derisively called "Churchianity" because it encourages people to attend a church but does not push them to live radically different lives. That is presented as extra credit or perhaps even as distasteful and fanatical. But that is not true Christian faith. Bonhoeffer saw this sort of cultural Christian faith in Germany and preached strongly against it. He knew that it was not sufficient to change souls and save the world, but that many church leaders were pretending that it was, and likely believed so themselves.

When the Bible says that we become "new creations" in Christ, it means that our whole lives will be given over to God and His purposes. This transformation will be different for each of us, but the principle is always the same. It is the joyful invitation that God makes possible for us. Therefore, how we do this cannot be reduced or distilled. There is a mystery to it. But often, we prefer to murder the mystery that is paradoxically bound up with the truth of God, dissect it into a handful of parts, and then have those dead parts nicely arranged for us. *Simply believe these creeds and perhaps do these few actions, and the rest of everything is all yours.* This false "religious" view of the faith presents a bare minimum as the standard, as though actually loving God with our whole hearts and minds and souls and bodies were a burden rather than a joy. It also puts forward the idea that what we say we believe intellectually doesn't need to be reflected in our whole lives, as though our intellectual assent is all that "faith" requires.

But "religion" can fail in the opposite direction, too. Just as it can make us essentially secular—apart from our few nonnegotiable "religious" activities which constitute the acceptable minimum—we can go to the opposite extreme, becoming religion-obsessed fanatics who nearly kill ourselves doing what we've been told must be done and thereby miss the freedom and joy of God. In these cases, the focus is again on our own efforts rather than on God's, and is simply moralism.

This was the worst of the high medieval church, which had almost comically boiled things down to a series of religious acts. *Here is the list of things you can do, and here is the list of things you cannot. Follow this, and you will be on a moral ladder leading you to Heaven.*

In some ways, Martin Luther is the ultimate example of this "religious" way of doing things. When he became a monk in the first years of the sixteenth century, he believed there was a crystal-clear road map to Heaven. But the process of living out his obsessive "monkery" became increasingly frustrating. He found that rather than causing him to love God more, it actually made him hate God—which is, of course, a clue that something is wrong. This is not to relegate the Roman Catholic faith to the corrupt caricature to which Luther subscribed at that particular period, but it gives us a picture of what can happen when we take the formula someone gives us and believe that we should work ourselves half-dead doing exactly what it says—that we can climb the ladder up to Heaven rung by rung and eventually get there. Most of us are never good enough at it to fool ourselves into thinking it might work.

But Luther was exceedingly good at it, so he had a rare opportunity to see that it really and truly doesn't work. He saw that obsessive religious activity was not the answer. As a result, he discovered within the pages of the Bible—which was not often read in the centuries preceding him—that the answer to his problems was simply having faith in Jesus, who had already achieved what we never could. It was a lightning-bolt revelation, and most would say it really did enable many to exchange the deadening shackles of what had been mere "religion" for the truth and joy of actually following God wholeheartedly.

But human nature is a funny thing. Just because Luther had seen the problem and corrected it for himself and some others did not mean that it was corrected forever. Human beings will always find new ways to fool themselves in new "religious" ways, and God in His mercy will always send His prophets to help them see how they have again fooled themselves.

Bonhoeffer was one of those prophets. He saw that in the four hundred years since Luther, so much emphasis had been put on being saved by faith and not by works that the idea of living out one's faith via works had been lost. As a result, the German church in the early 1930s had become flabby and essentially useless. When the evil of the Nazis came into culture, the church was not up to the job of heroically standing against it. They didn't have the faith necessary and therefore could not summon the will. And if we do not have the will to fight, we persuade ourselves that perhaps the prudent thing to do is make peace with our foes on the best terms possible.

Making Peace with Evil

In 334 BC, Alexander the Great landed his forces on the shore of what was then the great empire of Persia. He was going against as formidable a foe as conceivable, so in order to increase the odds of success, he did something so dramatic and wild that many would have considered it madness: He ordered his men to burn the boats in which they had traveled. Either they would fight and win, or they would die.

This episode in history reminds us of the inclination within every human heart to have an escape option. Why burn your boats when you might lose? Isn't it smarter to keep the option of a retreat open so that you might live to fight another day? Of course, that might be the prudent view. But there are other times when it really is wiser not to have an escape option, because when the going gets tough, we will almost certainly opt to escape rather than fight through. Not being open to divorce in one's marriage is like this. Statistics prove that couples who battle through the hardest parts of marriage—the very time when divorce may have seemed like the best option—often discover that weathering that particular difficulty strengthened their marriage in a way they could not have anticipated, and they are afterward glad that they didn't have the escape option open to them.

So what if that difficulty is the crucial point of the whole battle? And what if that battle is the crucial battle in the whole war? We know that Alexander's forces really did burn their boats and did not have the option of retreating to fight another day. We also know that they therefore fought with all their might and main. And we know that they won.

Of course, this is a martial illustration, but it is powerful for us. We know this was essentially what Bonhoeffer was hoping to communicate to the German church in his time. Either they would "burn their boats" and fight with all they had against the satanic evil of the Nazis, or they would certainly lose. But we know the German church did not fight with everything it had; rather, it dithered and made excuses for not fighting until it was too late. And we know the unprecedentedly horrifying results. Most German church leaders had dismissed Bonhoeffer as being overly dramatic. They believed it simply wasn't as bad as he said and that any efforts to do something about it wouldn't matter. Why should they risk everything? But they were wrong. And those who are failing to see that this is where we are in the American church are wrong, too.

One of the reasons the German church failed—and the American church is failing now—is because it failed to recognize the evilness of evil. If you do not recognize the genuine reality of what you are facing, you will certainly not risk everything in fighting it. Why would you? Why not make our peace with evil and take what terms we can get? The "religious" view foolishly thinks that coexisting with evil is possible. We do not see the real evilness of evil and do not understand that if we do not fight it, it will eventually consume us.

This illusion is related to the idea that the church should remain in its "theological" or "religious" sphere. Why not remain in our caves privately practicing our faith? Perhaps those outside will leave us alone and sometime in the future we can emerge to try again. But this is the perfect opposite of what real faith asks of us—which is to take our faith out of the merely religious sphere and into all the world. One is the seemingly safe and "prudent" path. It asks: "Why not keep some of our powder dry for tomorrow's battle?"

But what if there will be no battle tomorrow? What if this is the last battle?

If one realizes that we really are in an all-out war with evil and that God calls us to fight, then we are worse than fools not to do so. Indeed, God has called us to do so right now, just as He called the

German church to do. Bonhoeffer correctly diagnosed the situation in Germany and called the church to burn the boats and fight. They did not follow his advice, and lost everything.

Because we know what happened, will we hear what Bonhoeffer had to say? Or will we again dismiss it as fearmongering and retreat to our safe "religious" practices in our safe "religious" spheres?

The overwhelming tendency to see Bonhoeffer's view as overly dramatic is the result of what he rightly diagnosed as the secularization of our culture and the church. That is at the heart of what he saw as mere "religion."

CHAPTER FIVE

The Cautionary Tale of Martin Niemöller

I built the Third Reich!
You just worry about your sermons.

—Adolf Hitler, January 1934

W hen we consider how we might have behaved had we been living in Germany during the 1930s, we must consider the story of Martin Niemöller. As tempted as we are to think that we would have behaved like Dietrich Bonhoeffer, it is infinitely more likely that we would have behaved like Niemöller, who was a genuinely good man and a deeply committed Christian but who nonetheless misread the situation fatally. So if we are to avoid repeating his mistake, we must know and understand his story. As it stands now, many leaders in the American church are repeating his mistakes precisely, so his story could hardly be more important.

Knowing his story will help us see where we are today and hopefully help us repent before it's too late. It's already as close to too late as we can imagine. It will also help us to have grace for those who have made similar mistakes in our own time—including ourselves.

✳

Martin Niemöller was a proudly patriotic German born in 1892. He fought heroically in the First World War and earned the Iron Cross, First Class for his bravery as a submarine commander. After the war, he decided to become a Lutheran pastor. By the 1930s, he was the pastor of a prominent church in the affluent Berlin suburb of Dahlem.

Most of us know of the sickening evil the Nazis eventually perpetrated, but we must understand that most Germans, like Niemöller, could not possibly have foreseen these things. We must put ourselves in their shoes because we are essentially in their shoes today. If we flatter ourselves to think we would have behaved any differently than Niemöller, we must quickly disabuse ourselves of this fiction. That is our only real hope if we are to avoid his fatal mistakes.

Niemöller was a serious Christian and a deeply good man. He was patriotic in the best sense of the word and was one of that vast number of Germans who saw the results of the First World War as bitterly tragic and unfair to Germany. Few today would argue that Germany deserved the draconian measures imposed by the Allies in the Treaty of Versailles. And certainly for most Germans, the treaty's terms seemed calculated to humiliate them.

It should be noted that the United States did not sign the Versailles Treaty, and that the British economist John Maynard Keynes characterized its terms as unnecessarily harsh, saying they would ultimately be counterproductive. There can be no question that this proved true in the most dramatic terms imaginable. Only a few years after the treaty was signed, a certain Austrian corporal named Adolf Hitler began to leverage the powerful emotions of many Germans about this situation for his own political ends. Without his ability to do that, he never could have succeeded in gaining the power he did and ultimately perpetrating such evil.

So when Hitler appeared on the scene and appealed to the righteous indignation and pain most Germans felt, we can hardly be surprised that many turned in his direction. They saw in Hitler and his National Socialist movement a bright sign of hope for their future. And we must underscore that most Germans could not possibly have seen where Hitler really wanted to take them, and for us to pretend that we would have seen where things were headed under Hitler at that time is to engage in a self-aggrandizing fantasy.

For example, Soviet-style atheistic communism was a serious threat to Germany at that time, and Hitler brilliantly positioned himself as its sworn enemy. Of course, he did not admit that he was himself an atheist, or that he agreed with the Soviet communist idea that the state had ultimate authority, or that the American ideas of liberty and self-government were repulsive to him. Like many politicians, he said only what he needed to say to gain more power for himself. When the time was right and there was no danger to him, he could reveal who he really was and what he believed clearly enough. But why not let others believe what they liked in the meantime?

The patriotic pastor Martin Niemöller was one of the key figures Hitler cynically used to convince German Christians that when it came to issues of church and state, the Nazi movement was the very height of reasonableness. In late 1932, only months before Hitler became chancellor, he met with Niemöller and personally assured him that if he was elected, he would keep his hands off the church. Furthermore, he declared that he would not institute pogroms against the Jews.

Niemöller was put at ease by Hitler's assurances; he hardly could have imagined that Hitler was simply lying to him. But with the hindsight that we possess today, we know that Hitler was as far from a man of honor and character as we might ever imagine, and would say and do literally anything to gain power. We can also see how a man of genuine honor and character—as Niemöller was—would find it difficult to fathom that the head of the nation he loved would lie to his face, as Hitler did in that meeting, and would do the same with innumerable others throughout the grotesque arc of his life.

This first meeting between Niemöller and Hitler raises for us the issue of Jesus's words enjoining all of us to be "wise as serpents and gentle as doves." How many Christians today forget that Jesus cautioned us in this way and are naïve about evil just as Niemöller was? We may even think our innocence on this score to be some kind of virtue, as though being unable to fathom evil in others is somehow more Christian than seeing evil where it exists. But that's not how Jesus saw things, else He would not have said what He said. So if we think we are somehow more Christian than Jesus, we are in the most dire straits possible.

We might ask ourselves how we respond when an authority figure—whether a medical expert, politician, pastor, journalist, or anyone else—says something. Do we take the responsibility of weighing it carefully, heeding Jesus's warning to us about our fellow men and women? The Scriptures tell us that Jesus "knew what was in the heart of men." Do we agree with His assessment of human nature? If we do—and we cannot call ourselves Christians if we do not—we are to take evil seriously and not turn a blind eye to it, as easy and as convenient as that often may be for us. So while we may today forgive Niemöller's acceptance of Hitler's assurances at face value, we must also wonder when we ourselves have believed someone but perhaps should not have. When we have done this, have we, too, been guilty of helping evil along its path to power?

To direct the question at ourselves, we might think of the most controversial issues of our own time, when we were the most strongly tempted to unquestioningly go along with things we have been told. Did we believe those political or medical experts who told us that we should not question the efficacy or safety of experimental vaccines, and that for the sake of everyone, it was our duty as Christians to get those shots? When people were silenced for saying what they felt was important on this subject, did it set off alarm bells for us and goad us to speak out, or did it cause us to censor ourselves the more strongly? What was our duty to God? In going along with those things, were we being wise as serpents—or wise as doves?

Another tremendously controversial issue many in the church were tempted to remain silent about was the last presidential election. Did we believe that it was in the best interests of our country and the world not to question what appeared to millions of our fellow countrymen to be fraud of various kinds? Was it wise for us to accept the idea that questioning such things was somehow disloyal to the process or mere conspiracy theorizing? If we did go along with that narrative, why did we keep silent? Why did we not say that questioning such things was actually a sign of devotion to the ideas of self-government and democracy, and that to not question such things only shows naïveté concerning evil? What could the harm be in questioning either of these things if we really were interested in the truth of the matter? And what did it say about those telling us we must not question those things? Finally, if we did go along without questioning anything, what are we to do about it now?

We will come to that. But for now, let's continue with the story of Martin Niemöller.

Immediately after Hitler took power in early 1933, he did precisely what he had told Niemöller he would not do regarding the German church: He deputized those in power around him to push hard for the establishment of a German *Reichskirche*—a state church that would destroy the real German church and reflect Nazi values rather than Christian values. The Nazis wanted to control every single aspect of German society, and as far as they were concerned, the church was only a part of German society. Why should it be an exception?

This is the way totalitarians and statists always think: The church must bow to their authority, and they will take extreme measures in dealing with it. This was the case in the former Soviet Union and is today the case in China. Secularism—or actually, atheism—is the official religion of such regimes.

And so it was for Hitler and the Nazis. This was precisely what Bonhoeffer had warned against. Still, Niemöller was not ready to worry too much just yet. He believed that Hitler himself was not personally behind these developments and that others in his circle were the ones to blame. So as far as Niemöller saw it, this was not the time to take a strong and clear stand against the Nazis. Hitler could—and surely would—be reasonable; Niemöller flattered himself that he would use his influence with the Führer to see to it, and tried to arrange another meeting.

But getting this meeting was terribly difficult. It was scheduled and rescheduled, postponed again and again. Not until January 1934 did that meeting between Niemöller and Hitler finally take place. But the Hitler whom Niemöller would now meet was astonishingly different than the one who had given Niemöller his solemn assurances on the other side of his election to the German chancellorship fourteen months earlier.

Have we ourselves never heard of politicians who promise certain things before they are elected and then renege on those promises once in power? Many politicians far less wicked than Hitler have done so.

So when Niemöller was ushered into the chancellery that day, he would see what he had previously been too naïve to see and how very badly he had miscalculated the situation. In its way, it was something out of a nightmare, and what happened in that meeting dramatically and perfectly clarified for Niemöller how authoritarian secular forces regard the church. It was as sobering and chilling a lesson as we can imagine—and ought to be just as sobering and chilling a warning to us today.

Part of what made it so horrifying was Niemöller's optimism entering the meeting and then the shocking reality that confronted him. No sooner was Niemöller with Hitler and his top lieutenants than they revealed their true colors: Hermann Göring, who was a dedicated enemy of pastors like Niemöller, produced the transcript of a phone call that Niemöller had made and began reading what Niemöller had said, including some kind of joke about a meeting between Hitler and the elderly former president of Germany at that time.

When Göring read Niemöller's comments, Hitler exploded. "This is completely unheard of!" he shouted. "I will attack this rebellion with every means at my disposal!" Of course, Niemöller was utterly blindsided by this development. We now see that he had been ambushed. Hitler had no intention of having anything like a serious meeting with him to discuss church issues. He and his lieutenants only wished to terrorize and silence this upstart pastor. The whole point of the exercise was to let Niemöller know that he was already in trouble, and it was only due to Hitler's mercy that he wasn't in a concentration camp that minute.

Niemöller was horrified and frightened, and years later wrote of Hitler's angry raving: "I thought, what do I answer to all his complaints and accusations? He was still speaking, speaking,

speaking. I thought, dear God, let him stop."[1] Eventually, Niemöller tried to clarify the situation, still believing it all must be a great misunderstanding. He hoped to explain that he was indeed a loyal German and had meant no harm in whatever he had said.

"We are all enthusiastic about the Third Reich," he said, thinking this declaration might somehow assuage the irate Führer. But Hitler was long past receiving such a friendly and humble statement with the false graciousness that is the hallmark of the political operator. He was not interested in placating anyone in the church who was not already dancing to the tune he was playing. In part, it was as a result of Christian leaders like Niemöller, who had spent the last year giving Hitler the benefit of the doubt and not acting decisively and strongly against the Nazis' brazen trampling of the German church, that Hitler had no need to be conciliatory any longer. Niemöller and others had unwittingly given him the time and space to do all he needed to amass power and silence his enemies. So all Hitler was interested in doing from that point on was further consolidating power and doing as he liked. All he wished to do in that meeting was make sure that irritating Christian leaders like Niemöller were forevermore frightened into silence.

What Hitler then said is striking not just in its harshness, but in its perfect clarity regarding the larger situation. "I'm the one who built the Third Reich!" he fumed, obviously offended that anyone might dare to suggest it was anything that might call for collaboration. "You just worry about your sermons!"[2]

In other words, Hitler embodied the attitude of those who are the enemies of actual Christian faith, or what Bonhoeffer called "religionless Christianity." He made clear that the only sort of church he was interested in was one that never dared step beyond the religious corner assigned to it by the all-powerful state. In the Third Reich, the church had no business thinking it could take its ideas beyond that area. As we have said, that sort of church's faith is more like a mere hobby done in the basement that doesn't bother anyone outside. You do what you like in that building at such and such an hour on Sunday, and when you leave that building, you bow to the secular authority of the state.

But true Christianity cannot help but go beyond the boundaries of sermons—and beyond the boundaries of church buildings and services. This is its very essence. True Christianity knows no real boundaries because it is allied with Truth itself, which has no boundaries. And of course, those who follow Jesus and call Him Lord know He said that He Himself is the Truth. Therefore, Christian faith cannot, under any circumstances, confine itself to sermons or to Sunday mornings or to particular buildings—or to merely ecclesiastical or "religious" issues. It will inevitably touch on everything, as it is precisely God's will for it to do. It will have something to say about how a government operates and about every kind of issue—cultural, social, and otherwise. Bonhoeffer once said that the church was the "conscience of the state." So Christians could never keep silent on issues concerning the state. But Hitler in that signal moment made it perfectly clear that whatever illusion Niemöller might have harbored about the Christian church having any say whatever in the life of the Third Reich was a fantasy.

Hitler in his blunt statement perfectly clarified that version of the Christian faith—which is actually the devil's version and the only one acceptable to those authoritarian states that serve him and his purposes, however much they claim to be merely "secular" or even "atheistic." Whether run by mad tyrants like Hitler or Stalin in the past, or Kim Jong Un in our own day, or Muslim theocracies such as we find in Iran, the true Church and serious Christians are the enemy.

Such states have total authority and will brook no dissent, so the idea of a group of people who claim to have another view of anything is fundamentally unacceptable. Faith in any authority besides the state is absolutely unacceptable and must be crushed.

So Hitler was very happy to talk about "God" as long as that perverse version of "God" was on his side and served his purposes. And of course, he only spoke of God at all to keep the German people deluded into thinking that he had some genuine respect for the God of the Bible, which he obviously did not.

Very similarly, the Chinese Communist party will today designate "official" churches of which they approve. Of course, this is a deeply evil deception, because the devil's bargain they have made with these "churches" is that they will never dare to bring up anything at any time that in any way would counter the atheistic and authoritarian doctrines of the Communist regime. In other words, these churches have agreed not to be the Church in any real sense. They cannot even teach the actual Christian faith to their congregants, because that would make clear that the communistic regime in which they live is illegitimate.

In that January 1934 meeting with Hitler, Martin Niemöller finally understood that he had been fooled—and fooled very badly. If he had seen the reality of the situation and had been willing to stick his neck out earlier and join others in doing so, things might have gone differently. But that opportunity was past.

Nonetheless, after this unpleasant encounter, Niemöller was a different man. From that point forward, he spoke very bravely and clearly against the Nazis and did all he could to wake up anyone else still thinking all would be well if only they cooperated with the Third Reich. Later in 1934, along with Bonhoeffer and others, he founded the Confessing Church—which strongly opposed the Nazification of the German church and stood clearly against the Nazis and their policies.

But by then, it was essentially too late.

Things continued to get worse, and the church was persecuted increasingly strongly. At last, in July 1937, Niemöller was arrested. When he was released in March 1938, he was immediately rearrested by the Gestapo, who by that time could essentially do as they liked. From that time until the end of the war, he was interned in the concentration camps at Sachsenhausen and Dachau, and narrowly escaped with his life. Afterward, he wrote a rather famous poem, which we shall discuss in the next chapter.

But the question now comes to each of us: Are we able to admit we were wrong about something or someone, as Niemöller was able to do? Are we able to see that what we thought was genuine Christianity was perhaps tainted with mere "religion," and when push came to shove, did we see just how fatally tainted our Christianity was? Are we, like Niemöller, able to repent of our failure? Would we do so as publicly as he did?

Will we now?

CHAPTER SIX

The Spirit behind Cancel Culture

First they came for the Communists
and I did not speak out—
because I was not a Communist.

—Martin Niemöller

If we are putting forward the idea of "religionless Christianity" as the answer to the evil we are seeing around us, we should draw a picture of what that evil looks like. And at the dark heart of the evil we are seeing in our time lies that hideous thing called "cancel culture." Most of us have experienced something of "cancel culture," or we have at least seen it in operation around us. It works roughly as follows.

Someone says something that someone else—it's never quite clear who—deems to be beyond the pale. "Marriage is between a man and a woman for life." "There are only two sexes, and a man cannot become a woman." "The COVID vaccines are not helpful, but harmful." "The election was stolen, and we should investigate it." "The Bible is the Word of God." Any of these statements, and many others, are all it takes. Before we know it, a kind of mob mentality takes over in which the person who made the statement is condemned over and over in the harshest terms. Anyone who might be inclined to stand up for the attacked person is pressured to say nothing, lest they too be attacked. Pressure is also put upon anyone associated with that person to publicly disassociate themselves from him or her; if you don't do that, the mob may well come for you, too.

Fear is always at work in this dynamic. It has nothing to do with real justice. The mob who is doing this is never defined, but we can feel that the spirit animating this process is malevolent. Therefore, it is not interested in actual justice. Though it will toss around terms like "justice" and "equality" to deceive people, it actually does not believe in these things at all.

Nor is there ever an impartial group to whom the attacked person can appeal who might judge the situation coolly and wisely. There is only a mob with a mob mentality, and of course, this is all exacerbated and magnified by social media.

The spirit behind cancel culture is genuinely evil and markedly anti-Christian. It is a devouring spirit that knows no mercy. Indeed, it is at war with God's ideas of grace, mercy, and forgiveness. Even when the "offending" person grovels toward offering some kind of apology, those animated by the spirit of cancel culture are neither forgiving nor kind and never treat the offending party with anything resembling grace. That would go against the spirit of the whole affair. An example must be made, and those who are watching must be appropriately terrorized, lest they speak out, too.

The spirit animating cancel culture today is the same spirit that has operated throughout history, and at least since the French Revolution in the 1790s. It was also in full operation during the nightmare of the Chinese Cultural Revolution in the 1960s, when people were publicly shamed and humiliated as a matter of course. Anyone familiar with either of these revolutions can see that what we are dealing with is not merely secular or atheistic, but genuinely satanic. Cruelty and unforgiveness are two of its chief characteristics.

In the French Revolution, when countless thousands were condemned and then beheaded for their crimes against the "Revolution," it was called the "Reign of Terror." No one was safe. Those who were doing the beheading might themselves be accused, and then they too would be beheaded. There was no standard by which to measure anything objectively—or if there was a standard at one moment, it might change in the next. Abject fear and madness reigned.

We have seen this spirit again and again since then. It was prominently at work in the Soviet Bolshevik Revolution and afterward under the satanic despotism of Joseph Stalin. When he was at the helm, no one could ever be too careful, and even those who were the most careful of all were often hauled away, never to be seen again. For a half-hearted joke in a letter to a friend, the great Aleksandr Solzhenitsyn was condemned to the Siberian prison camps of the Gulag, where he suffered and witnessed the unbearable evils he wrote about in his book *The Gulag Archipelago*.

This spirit was, of course, at work in Nazi Germany. In Niemöller's January 1934 meeting with Hitler, a single harmless remark was held up as the most outrageous and offensive thing imaginable. One might—like Niemöller—have given a lifetime of service to his country and, by every impartial account, have been a good and a noble person. But all of that is wiped away, and the single "sin" is held up as all the evidence needed to condemn the accused. We would do well to recognize the satanic voice of "the Accuser" in these instances. It is about accusation only, and there can never be any redemption. It is hopelessness writ large, as over the entrance to Dante's Inferno.

We have seen this at work in America in our own time, and only need reference the insane lie of the 1619 Project. This was not only commissioned and pushed by the once venerable and respected *New York Times*, but even won a Pulitzer Prize—which, like the Nobel Prize, once stood at the acme of how we decided what was laudable. But we are living in a new day and are obliged to wake up to where we are, lest we ourselves become passive promoters of the evil. We now must acknowledge that these "elite" institutions have abandoned whatever noble principles once guided them. They are now working hand in glove with the enemies of objective truth, and are handmaidens to these evils.

At the heart of the 1619 Project is the lunatic and wicked idea that the United States was founded by racists to further racism—and that this sin can never be expunged. The fundamental assertions which the author makes are untrue, but this is not the place to explicate how dramatically false they are. Suffice it to say, they are not merely wrong, but are wrong in a way that is intentionally malevolent. I point this out to make clear that the spirit behind the assertions and the whole false narrative is a dark and accusing one that—like the spirits behind cancel culture—is diametrically opposed to God's idea of grace. In this case, it is connected to the world of so-called intersectionality and the "perpetual victim" mentality. Those in this perverse universe rejoice in being able to declare themselves oppressed and victimized, which they view as badges of the greatest honor. But because of this, they are not at all interested in actually changing whatever "injustices" they perceive and claim, but are mostly interested in punishing those whom they accuse of perpetrating them.

Those people talk loudly about wanting to change things but have no actual standard toward which they are moving. The idea of a standard of "justice" or "equality" is only an illusion they wish to present, but in reality, their goal is to be perpetually complaining, no matter what "progress" is made. Also, to actually—and perhaps graciously and gratefully—admit that some progress has been made over the decades is forbidden in these circles. To say that we have made progress on race would be seen as betraying the principles of the "perpetual Revolution." The complaining and the shrieking and the keening must be kept up. Never admit success or victory of any kind.

For example, it is unacceptable to celebrate the fact that America ended slavery more than 160 years ago, or to admit that more than six hundred thousand white men died in the war over that issue. It is frowned upon to say that the civil rights movement successfully ended Jim Crow laws. The normal and healthy expression that comes in celebrating these actual victories is denied, and a withering and endlessly complaining attitude is adopted instead. And we must never dare to mention that it was Christians who were principally behind the abolition movement in England and America, or that the civil rights movement came out of the American churches.

In the 1619 Project especially, we see that its advocates are principally concerned not with redeeming and bettering things, but with accusing and cursing those they see as the perpetrators, and with cursing America entirely. So just as someone might viciously say to a child, "You are just like your father!" or "You will never amount to anything! You're bad to the bone and always will be!" what they proclaim about America is the very definition of a curse and a "negative confession" (to use a term popular in some Christian circles). To those moved by this wicked spirit, the idea that one might change and become better is unacceptable in principle.

What we see at work here is a satanic spirt of accusation and cursing. Therefore, it is fatalistic, nihilistic, and the very definition of hopeless. This is precisely the way cancel culture and atheistic cultural Marxism work. It is not about making actual progress, but rather about a perpetual revolution. These things are not merely secular or even merely atheistic; they are aggressively anti-God and have a bitter and warlike hatred of God's values. Therefore, the spirit of cancel culture always operates in environments that are openly anti-God. The French Revolution was viciously and explicitly opposed to the

Church and murdered thousands of nuns and monks and priests. And
in the manifestations of this spirit that we saw in the twentieth
century, it was always within atheistic totalitarian "revolutions" in
Soviet Russia, Nazi Germany, and Communist China.

And now in America, we are seeing it again.

Although here we are not yet officially subjects of any openly
Marxist and atheistic regime, we nonetheless see that the spirit behind
cancel culture and much of the "revolution" of our own time openly
allies itself with cultural Marxism and atheism. We have never before
in America seen antipathy toward God and His values so openly and
decisively displayed. Whenever such things have been part of our
checkered history—whether in vigilante mobs or lynching mobs or
other manifestations—the phenomenon has been localized and always
condemned. But today, we are seeing this spirit assert itself across our
country in a way that is simply and undeniably unprecedented. Where
are the Christian voices in our culture condemning these evil things?
Why are so many in churches being silent, as though these things do
not directly concern them?

As we have said, these are the same spirits behind the rise of Nazism.
There was a menacing pagan atmosphere in the Nazi movement, and the
closer one got to the center of it, as in the SS, the more one saw open
occultism. The effect of this on Germans was predictable. It was
frightening. Anyone who spoke out likely would be sent to a concentration
camp, so it wasn't long before almost no one did.

In *Letter to the American Church*, I discussed this phenomenon
as the "Spiral of Silence," in which people who are silent on an issue
invariably help to silence others. No one wants to stick out and be the
one who is cancelled next, so everyone errs on the side of "caution"
and is silent, thereby guaranteeing that the forces of evil continue to
wreak their havoc. So what can we do about it?

To answer that question, we must return to the story of Martin
Niemöller.

CHAPTER SEVEN

Further Thoughts on Cancel Culture

After realizing his early errors and speaking out very bravely, pastor Martin Niemöller was arrested by the Nazis and spent eight years in concentration camps. At the end of the war, he managed to escape and so lived to tell the tale of what he had experienced. In 1947, he wrote his famous poem, which is so often quoted in our own time.

First they came for the Communists
and I did not speak out—
because I was not a Communist.
Then they came for the Socialists
and I did not speak out—
because I was not a Socialist.
Then they came for the trade unionists
and I did not speak out—
because I was not a trade unionist.
Then they came for the Jews

and I did not speak out—
because I was not a Jew.
Then they came for me—
and there was no one left
to speak out for me.

We can see now that what Niemöller was describing in this poem is precisely what we today call "cancel culture." We have seen it operating throughout history, as we have mentioned, and now in our own time. We cannot help noticing that it grows in power as it devours its victims. In the beginning, it isn't so dramatic, but over time, it demands more and more and more. It is never sated and cannot ever be, because it exists to accrue power and to destroy anything that gets in its way. So the more we do or say nothing against it, the more power we allow it to amass, until at last it comes for us.

Over the last few years, we have seen how the boundaries of what we can and cannot say have grown increasingly constricted. This is how the perpetual revolution works. We are very far from where we were only a few years ago, when there were still some "reasonable" voices—before everyone was afraid to speak out, lest they lose everything.

As we have said, the evil spirit that animates cancel culture is at war with truth itself, so it cannot have any genuine objective standards or any actual sense of justice. It will change what it demands as it progresses, just as someone addicted to a drug must have more of it, and then harder drugs, as time goes by. There is never enough.

We have seen this clearly over the last decade.

For example, in early 2012, my friend Kirk Cameron appeared on Piers Morgan's CNN program where, in the kindest and gentlest way imaginable, he discussed his support of marriage between a man and a woman.[1] One can hardly conceive how anyone could have phrased things more graciously, and he was only voicing what billions around the world believe—and certainly what every serious Jew, Christian, and Muslim has always believed. But that didn't matter. The powers that be in the culture had at some point decided that what he said was now "hateful," so he had to be demonized as an intolerant bigot. A litany of Hollywood celebrities, including his former *Growing Pains* costars, rounded on him; one very prominent Hollywood figure even went so far as to tweet that Cameron's comments made him "an accomplice to murder."[2]

But the larger question is: Where were all the Christian leaders who should have been defending him? Most of them didn't say a word, lest they be attacked too. Why not simply stay quiet and let Kirk Cameron take the heat? *Let the cultural forces devour him, and maybe they will leave us alone.* This is the idea expressed in the phrase "the devil take the hindmost." It is the idea that if we are being chased, we only need to outrun one person slower than we are so that they will be attacked and we can continue unharmed. This was Martin Niemöller's calculation. But he came to see the horror of his silence and publicly confessed it to the world in that poem and many other places.

What about the prominent Christian leaders of our own time?

Is there any doubt that the same dynamic at work under the Nazis is at work among us today? The silence of Christian leaders enables the juggernaut of cancel culture to continue amassing power. Today's world is far from the quaint culture of 2012. Today the issue is the patently insane idea that a man can become a woman, or a woman can become a man. And it is because Christian leaders were silent when Kirk Cameron bravely and graciously said what he said about homosexuality being unnatural and why marriage should not be redefined to include it—which most of them undoubtedly believed—that the door has been opened to every hellish idea we can imagine. We now live in a world where teachers are encouraging little children to ignore their loving parents and pursue hormone therapies and surgeries that will forever make it impossible for them to be the men and women God intended for them to be.

We had a moment to defend truth, but most of the Christian leaders failed to do so. Why did they keep silent?

Again, we return to the story of Martin Niemöller to see how it happened in his day, according to the poem he wrote repenting of it.

We remind ourselves that Niemöller was no coward. He had risked his life many times for his country during the First World War—and once he saw the true nature of Hitler and the Nazi movement, he was extremely brave in speaking out. But why did he not speak out before it was too late?

Obviously it was because he had no idea that his silence would lead to what it did. He had thought that preserving himself was probably the wisest course. His thinking was, "Let the Nazis go after the Communists! What does that matter to me?" Didn't the Communists have it coming, after all? Why should Niemöller have a problem with the Nazis going after those he himself saw as atheistic madmen who had taken over the formerly Christian country of Russia, and who were at that time trying to take over the rest of the world, one country at a time?

But what did not occur to Niemöller was that the Nazis were in many ways no different than the Soviet Communists. Even today we pretend that the Nazis were somehow on the extreme right and call them "fascists" instead of Communists or Socialists, whom we put on the extreme left. But of course, the term "Nazi" is only a shortened version of "National Socialist," and in their way, they agreed dramatically with the Communist version of things. Just like the Soviet Bolsheviks, whom they demonized as their bitterest enemies, they believed in the utter authority of the state and only used "God" language to deceive anyone in Germany who opposed the Communist atheists. We now know that the Nazis were every bit as atheistic as the Communists and every bit as authoritarian. The Nazis didn't ultimately believe in anything but their own power, and anything that was a threat to that power had to be crushed. Therefore, anything they needed to say to gain power must be said. And they fooled many, with Martin Niemöller at the head of that list.

We must understand again that what we are dealing with ultimately, in all these cases, is evil. It believes in nothing at all but its own power. It has no standards or principles because that would mean bowing to something outside itself. Those who worship power will never do that, but will play word games to fool people into thinking they have some ethical or moral standards guiding their behavior. Anyone who has had the experience of participating in an exorcism or a deliverance knows this is exactly how demons operate. There is no truth in them; they say anything that needs to be said to retain their power and place.

At first—in April 1933—the Nazis wiped out their enemies who called themselves Communists, not because they differed very much in their ideas but simply because there was no room for other ideas or other sources of power. Hitler had put himself forward as the answer to the problem of the Communists, and now he would deliver. But after this, the Nazis cracked down on the Socialists too, because while that term was in the very name the Nazis had taken themselves, they were not about to let anyone else in any other group share their power or try to tell them how they should govern. So any self-proclaimed Socialists who were not utterly pro-Nazi had to be wiped out. Then in May 1933, the Nazis brutally cracked down on the German trade unions. Anyone advocating for any kind of working standards or wages would at some point oppose what the Nazis had in mind, and that could not be tolerated.

Niemöller may not have liked the fact that the Nazis were doing these things, but was it really worth sticking his neck out? What did it matter in the bigger picture if the Nazis cracked down on the trade unionists? Niemöller saw the Church as the central issue in German culture, and as long as the Nazis didn't bother that, what did it matter to him? As long as he was able to have a voice in the National Socialist state and perhaps help guide Hitler, all might still be well.

But after eight years in concentration camps, Niemöller saw the truth and says in his poem that if you did not stand up in the beginning for those being persecuted—whether you agreed with them on everything or not—you were preparing the way for your own persecution. And of course, that is precisely what happened. When he finally saw it, it was too late. His own "silence in the face of evil" had made it all possible because he had failed to discern the spirit behind what was happening. If he had done so, he would have stood up for others on principle.

This is why we today must stand with anyone and everyone who is being cancelled. A foundational principle is being violated. The idea that we have free speech and must tolerate different views lies at the heart of all our liberties.

The example of Martin Niemöller should chill us to the core, because not only did he—a genuinely good Christian man—make this fatal mistake, but he saw the effects of his mistake play out by enabling the Third Reich to wreak evil upon millions. Far worse, he wrote about it to warn us never to repeat the same mistake—and yet, what Christian leader has quoted this poem to strengthen the Church to stand with those who today are being devoured by the spirit of cancel culture? None come to mind.

It is not enough for us to stand with those with whom we agree who are being attacked, as every Christian leader ought to have stood with Kirk Cameron, for example. But we must also stand on principle with anyone who is being attacked in this way. We must discern the spirit behind the canceling and know that it is at war with God's ideas of mercy and justice and grace. It is also at war with the American idea of liberty, for which millions of patriots have died. That idea of liberty is God's idea of liberty. We must not be afraid to acknowledge that all the best ideas throughout history have their roots in God; therefore, we can understand that those who are at war with the American ideals of freedom of speech and freedom of religion are at war with God, because standing up for free speech and freedom of religion is what God calls us to do. It is extraordinary to think that many Americans who are not Christians nonetheless understand the sanctity of these ideas and are willing to defend them.

Many of us of a certain age will remember something often quoted in years past, which I remember hearing in college: "I may disagree with what you say, but I will defend to the death your right to say it." This is a wonderful expression of this foundational American idea. (It is often attributed to Voltaire, though it is doubtful he said it.) Nonetheless, this biblical idea found its way to Enlightenment thinkers like Voltaire and was eventually enshrined in our founding documents. Indeed, it is in the very first amendment to our Constitution:

> Congress shall make no law respecting an establishment
> of religion, or prohibiting the free exercise thereof; or
> abridging the freedom of speech, or of the press; or the
> right of the people peaceably to assemble, and to petition
> the Government for a redress of grievances.

As we have said, this idea ultimately came to us from the Bible—most notably through Martin Luther, who affirmed the necessity of people answering first to God for their beliefs and actions and not merely to some powerful authority—and then through several Enlightenment voices until it became a part of our official American laws.

Those who went after Kirk Cameron were less concerned with what he said than the idea that he would dare say anything that did not go along with their views. They had to make an example of him and banked on the fact that if they did it strongly enough, most of his fellow Christians would say nothing. Of course, they were right. And the moment they had done that, they set their sights on the next one who would dare speak out.

The spirit behind cancel culture is one that is all about power and which is at war with anything that challenges it. It is an antichrist spirit. It has no fidelity to anything except itself. It will spout platitudes about anything that might help it make some progress in accruing power, which is its only goal. So if talking about racism can move the ball forward, it will talk about racism, and anyone may be deemed "racist" for any reason. If talking about any marginalized group can move the ball forward, it will talk about marginalized groups. But we must repeat that there is no actual principle or standard at work, so any reasons the spirit piously and forthrightly gives are inevitably false, and we must stop being fooled. Those who champion these things will spout platitudes but will conveniently forget them if those platitudes get in the way of amassing power. The devil has no principles.

To see this dynamic, we only need to go back to Kirk Cameron and everyone being put on notice that the biblical view of marriage would no longer be tolerated. Suddenly everyone who had a biblical view of marriage—which President Barack Obama and nearly every other Democrat had espoused—was silenced or cast as being against "love" and therefore a proponent of "hate." There was no principled discussion of the actual merits of the issue, or of whether children would be better served with both a mother and a father. Real discussion was shut down, because proponents of same-sex marriage knew that if a real discussion were to be had, they would lose. So they embraced the cancel culture on that issue, and we have reaped the whirlwind ever since. Now many gay people who well-meaningly advocated for same-sex marriage find that they are themselves being demonized if they don't go along with the madness of the trans movement, including providing pornographic homosexual material to children.

Many who didn't mind the idea of gay people being able to marry nonetheless raised the question of what would happen to those who opposed same-sex marriage if it did indeed become legal. Would the government begin to coerce people to violate their religious liberty and conscience? This was a very serious issue. But these serious concerns were mocked as being beside the point. And indeed, the moment same-sex marriage was legalized, the religious liberties of those who dissented were attacked. Those opposed to it were increasingly forced to agree with it publicly and to celebrate it. What had one moment been cast as a private matter that wouldn't concern or harm anyone else was immediately cast as a public issue because the goalposts had been moved. When a baker declined to bake a cake for a same-sex wedding because he felt it violated his conscience, he was sued by the state of Colorado. Up to that point, same-sex marriage advocates had cast their cause as an issue of "live and let live," but once it became legal, the "live and let live" argument suddenly didn't apply to that baker. He was vilified as a hatemonger and not allowed to hold the very views that every U.S. president had held until a few years before.

But again, we must note that the proponents of these movements do not subscribe to any foundational principles. They simply want to win, and will say whatever is necessary at the time. They are not concerned with truth or justice or liberty—only with power.

And this brings us to where we are today. The free speech and religious liberties enshrined in our founding documents to protect everyone in our nation are increasingly being shoved aside—and any previous accommodations that might have been talked about in 2015 for people of faith before the U.S. Supreme Court legalized same-sex marriage nationwide are brusquely ignored, or worse than that, sneered at as beneath contempt. This is the spirit of cancel culture at work. The German church failed to discern these things as the Nazis rose to power and Bonhoeffer's warnings fell on deaf ears. We have an opportunity to discern them now. But will we?

So we ask: Is your pastor speaking openly about these things? Is he standing with those who are being silenced and exhorting you to do the same? Or does he prefer to let others take the heat, making the excuse that he is called to "stay in his lane" and not bring his faith into these other spheres as so many German pastors did? If this is the case, you must yourself repent of calling him your pastor and find another church. Otherwise, you are complicit in his silence and share his guilt before God. Do you trust God enough to do that? Will you do that? The hour is late.

"Religionless Christianity" obliges us to stand bravely for these ideas seminal to genuine freedom and to stand against the demonic spirits that oppose it.

CHAPTER EIGHT

Some Religious Idols

He also told this parable to some who trusted in themselves
that they were righteous, and treated others with contempt:
"Two men went up into the temple to pray, one a Pharisee
and the other a tax collector. The Pharisee, standing by
himself, prayed thus: 'God, I thank you that I am not like
other men, extortioners, unjust, adulterers, or even like this
tax collector. I fast twice a week; I give tithes of all that I
get.' But the tax collector, standing far off, would not even
lift up his eyes to heaven, but beat his breast, saying, 'God,
be merciful to me, a sinner!' I tell you, this man went down
to his house justified, rather than the other. For everyone
who exalts himself will be humbled, but the one who
humbles himself will be exalted."

—Luke 18:9–14

When we talk about "religionless Christianity" as true faith in Jesus, we see that to be "religious" is not merely to miss the mark, as when we sin. Rather, it is something especially and deeply wicked. It is to pretend to be doing something for God when we are in fact standing against God and His will. Jesus's frightening condemnation of the Pharisees and other religious leaders of His day shows us in no uncertain terms what He thought of the outward display of "religion" when it is divorced from, and even opposed to,

God's will. In the Gospel of John, Jesus says to some of the most dedicatedly religious men of His day:

> You are of your father the devil, and your will is to do your father's desires. He was a murderer from the beginning, and does not stand in the truth, because there is no truth in him. When he lies, he speaks out of his own character, for he is a liar and the father of lies. But because I tell the truth, you do not believe me. (John 8:44–45)

No one was more religious than the people to whom Jesus directed these chilling words. The Pharisees and other religious leaders were known to be as outwardly "respectable" as one could imagine. They were not known to be "sinners" in any way. They were not known to be adulterers or in any way sexually promiscuous and did not say coarse things in public, nor probably in private either. They knew the Scriptures inside and out, prayed publicly, and performed religious sacrifices in the way they believed to be proper, even down to the extraordinary and perhaps preposterous length of tithing herbs. They therefore held themselves out as models of what it meant to be faithful to God, often to the point of ostentation. Yet Jesus repeatedly condemned them in the strongest possible terms as hypocrites and liars whose hearts were far from God.

Of course, most of the Pharisees were dedicatedly opposed to Jesus, pointedly condemning Him as insufficiently "religious" and a troublemaker, generally. His actions and words seemed a rebuke to all that they did and said—and they were. The Pharisees were shocked that Jesus consorted with "gluttons and wine-bibbers," prostitutes, and tax collectors because they themselves wouldn't go near such people and obviously prided themselves on this. But what may be of most interest to us today is that Jesus's public denunciations of these religious leaders were scorching, as though calculated to enrage them.

This brings us to one of the religious idols of our day: the idol of winsomeness. Is it possible that Jesus did not understand that He was to be winsome at all times? There is also something we might call an idol of unity. Did Jesus not care about unity with His religious brethren and only wish to divide Himself and His followers from them? Renouncing these powerful religious leaders as being "of their father the devil" was not at all winsome. Nor was calling them a "brood of vipers" and "white-washed tombs full of dead men's bones" helpful toward unity. Yet if we believe Jesus was the sinless Son of God, as Christians must, then we are obliged to agree that His assessment of these leaders and the withering way in which he expressed that assessment were absolutely perfect. Are we not to follow in these footsteps of His, or does our version of the Christian faith put itself forward as more holy than Jesus Himself?

What Jesus condemned so strongly in the religious leaders of his day was, of course, their "religiosity" along precisely the lines we are discussing. Not only did He not praise them for their moral uprightness, but He caustically used it against them, saying that it was actually evil because it was meant to deceive God about the real condition of their hearts toward Him. This brings us to another idol, which we might call the idol of respectability. The Pharisees' outward respectability was anathema to Jesus, and He said so in a way that was not calculated to appear in any way respectable or winsome.

But here is the difficult question: Can we in the Christian church imagine that we might be guilty of the very same "religious" behavior as those whom Jesus condemned? Or do we think it was only the religious leaders of that time whom He would condemn in this way? Do we think that because they were Jewish and rejected Jesus as the

Messiah that they were guilty in a way that we cannot be? Of course, if religious leaders in our own day are guilty of these things, they needn't look like the pious moralistic religious leaders of Jesus's day. They will have other religious idols they worship.

But let's start with what many Christian religious leaders—and other Christians—may have in common with the religious leaders of Jesus's day. Let us begin with the idol of respectability.

Respectability is usually a good thing. In many places in the Scriptures, God calls us to be respectable in our behavior. For example, Romans 12:18 enjoins us to "be at peace with all men," as far as that is possible. We are not to be rabble-rousers and troublemakers and so insistent on "truth" to the extent that we are perpetually at war with everyone around us. Romans 13:1 tells us that we are to "obey the governing authorities." So our general attitude toward government should be one of respect. And of course, 1 Thessalonians 5:22 tells us to "abstain from every form of evil," so that even if we are doing no evil, we aren't supposed to ignore the fact that how we appear to others will affect whether they are drawn to the God we worship or pushed away. So even the mere appearance of respectability is something we need to take seriously.

But like so many good things, we can make an idol of respectability, and when Jesus calls us away from it, we may sin by choosing outward respectability over obeying Him. We may have a disposition toward respectability, just as someone else might have a disposition toward rebellion—or to adultery or violence. We may never really feel tempted to do anything that might appear radical or "excessive," even if God is leading us in that direction for His purposes. So we may simply avoid doing what God is asking us to do because it has a certain wildness or indecorousness to it that we are not used to.

But whatever our fundamental disposition, there may be times when God calls us to do something that doesn't seem "respectable," and that will be difficult for many of our Christian brethren to understand, especially those who are the most "religiously" inclined. So we need real discernment. Bonhoeffer faced this in particular, as we shall see.

Scripture offers numerous examples of God's heroes not acting in a perfectly respectable way. We have already quoted Jesus, who was attacked by the religious leaders of His time for behaving in a way that didn't seem right to them. Most famously, they accused Him of consorting with sinners, which in their view was not at all respectable. And as we have said, Jesus said many things that were shocking and not very "respectable." Everywhere we look in the gospels, we see Jesus doing things that struck the religious leaders as out-of-bounds.

So how is it that many Christians have adopted this attitude of "respectability" as though it were at the very heart of Jesus's most fundamental teachings? How is it that they are modeling this posture for Christians in the public sphere? Are there not times when we must speak out boldly and risk the obloquy of others? Tragically, many Christian leaders today are so "religious" that they are more like those whom Jesus excoriated than like Jesus Himself, who at times appeared quite wild. But if we wish to follow Jesus as our model, we see that there is a time to dandle little children on our laps, and there is a time to turn over tables in the temple. We see that there is a time to be gentle toward those with whom we disagree, and there is a time to thunder at them.

Much of the problem we face today in our "religiosity" is that we have been given a false choice. We seem to think that the opposite of being an openly sinful and irreligious person is to be an outwardly respectable and "religious" person. But we know Jesus condemned the latter far more than the former. He was calling people to something else. It was not a choice between being an immoral sinner and being a morally upright "religious" person; He was calling everyone to Himself who did not fit either of these categories. This infuriated the most religious figures of His day, because He was criticizing their religiosity even more than He was criticizing the "sinfulness" of the sinners.

As we have said, "religious" behavior in this negative sense is not "openly sinful." On the contrary, it means setting up a "religious" idol to worship in place of God. That idol is usually an impressive counterfeit of God, because it is designed to appear to be a genuinely good thing, and even to masquerade as a holy thing. So those who claim to be Christians will be especially tempted to worship it. The devil hardly expects to succeed in tempting Christians by openly declaring who he is and what he stands for. On the contrary, in order to lure Christians away from true faith in Christ, he must come to us as "an angel of light."

We have already mentioned the idol of winsomeness, which is related to this idea of being "respectable" at all times. At some point in the last twenty years, it became fashionable to talk about Christians being winsome, as though this were a clear commandment from the mouth of Jesus—or even one that had been etched in the tablets of the Mosaic Law. Of course, generally speaking, being winsome is a laudable goal, and we should be winsome when possible, just as we generally ought to be "respectable" and "at peace with all men" to the degree that it depends on us. But at some point, as per the scriptural qualification "where it is possible," we realize it may at some point become impossible—and at that point, we are not to be at peace with all men.

But because we may rarely have come to that point, we may well have forgotten that it ever existed. But according to the Scriptures, it does, and we need to recognize it, lest we "be at peace" with those with whom we are not to be at peace. Do we think that we are called to "be at peace" with those who are openly preaching against what we know to be God's biblical commands? Are we afraid to be called "divisive" or "fundamentalist" or "unsophisticated" for saying what we know the Bible makes clear? Are we afraid of being accused of being "unwinsome"?

How has this "religious" and unbiblical idea of perpetual "winsomeness" entered the thinking of most serious Christians? Don't these otherwise good things—being respectable and winsome—sometimes tempt us away from saying exactly what God would want us to say?

Since we are on the subjects of respectability and winsomeness, have we forgotten how the prophet Elijah mocked the priests of Baal? Many Christians today firmly believe that mockery cannot be consonant with following God. But the Scriptures in this story give us an example of someone whose mocking was so sarcastic and almost vicious that we have no choice but to see that our view is entirely and embarrassingly mistaken. Is it not obvious from those passages that God approved of Elijah's mockery? And of the wild way in which he expressed himself?

Shall we forget that John the Baptist and Jesus also used mocking language? Mocking someone as they did is not winsome. But how can we believe we are always and everywhere to eschew such wild and mocking behavior? Do we have some tortured theological argument by which we can sequester the harsh words of Jesus, John the Baptist, and others so that they are no longer possibilities for how God might have us behave today? Have we forgotten the language that David used in addressing Goliath?

"This day the LORD will deliver you into my hand, and I
will strike you down and cut off your head. And I will give
the dead bodies of the host of the Philistines this day to the
birds of the air and to the wild beasts of the earth, that all
the earth may know that there is a God in Israel." (1 Samuel
17:46)

Nor was his following through on this in killing Goliath and
beheading him an act of winsomeness. Have we forgotten that
sometimes God calls us to be like David? Or have we become too
"religious" to imagine such a thing?

The enemy of our souls, in his craftiness, is always seeking where
he might tempt us with a religious idol—something that we are
persuaded is worth worshiping but which is actually a satanic substitute
for God, meant to subtly draw us away from worship of the one true
God. At the center of many such counterfeits is the idol of respectability.

Sometimes it is simply the sin of pride that causes us to worship
these idols of "respectability" and "winsomeness." We may pride
ourselves on not being like those embarrassing Christians we see
portrayed in the media who reject science and reason and good taste.
We attend a church where the pastor quotes the *New York Review
of Books* and hobnobs with writers at the *New York Times* and
Washington Post. Of course, to some extent, there may be nothing
wrong with this. To some extent, this actually may be God's will,
because we really do want to reach out to people for whom these
things may have value. But at what point have we merely given in to
the temptation toward pride—or power—so that we have been subtly
drawn away from serving God and His purposes? If we have invested
a great deal in creating a respectable portrait of ourselves—and
Christians in general—at what point does that investment pull us

away from God and God's will for us? Again, we will not be surprised to see that Bonhoeffer faced this difficulty.

To bring things painfully home, we may raise the specter of politics. What if we believe that supporting a certain candidate will be the best thing for the nation at this time because that candidate most likely has the best policies regarding things that matter to us, such as religious liberty, abortion, crime, and immigration? But if we are in a circle that frowns upon that candidate for a host of reasons, many of which may be valid, will we be able to follow our convictions, or does our concern for appearing "respectable" in our community overwhelm our ability to do so?

What if we simply hold an opinion that would make certain people change their good opinion of us? Are we to shrink from speaking the truth as we see it because we might lose their high esteem? Sometimes God really does call us to flee from this idea of respectability and trust Him with the consequences. Will we obey? Dare we admit that we have sometimes gone along with the crowd out of fear? Shall we disobey God in this way and think He doesn't mind?

The Idol of Purity

Related to these ideas is what we might call an idol of purity. This comes closer to what we observe in the scribes and Pharisees of Jesus's day. It is the temptation to say that above all else, I must keep my hands clean. I must not allow myself to become soiled in any way. The state of my own soul is all that matters. It matters more that I am "pure" than what might happen to others if I do something I think might "dirty my hands."

The idol of purity is a powerful one. Bonhoeffer faced this a great deal among the believers of his time. So let's ask ourselves, if we were living in Germany in the 1930s, and the Gestapo came to our door to ask if we were hiding a Jew—and we were—would we say yes? Do we believe that telling this lie is worse than allowing the Jew to be dragged away by the Gestapo? Do we really believe that we are only doing our duty to God, and that the Jew's fate is in God's hands and not ours?

To again bring up the unpleasant example of politics, we may again ask whether, like the Pharisees, we appear to be outwardly pure but disregard "doing justice and mercy" by refraining from voting for someone who fails to live up to our moral standards. According to Bonhoeffer, God sees that in this inaction, we are abdicating our responsibility toward the future. We are pretending there is a third way out—to vote for no one, as though that choice clears us of having allowed whoever is elected into office, whose policies will affect millions. Again, do I have no responsibility to my fellow citizens on this score?

Is our responsibility before God to "do justice" regarding our fellow citizens not more important than wishing to appear above the filthy political fray of pulling the lever for someone many might think unpleasant? Do we believe that we will win someone to faith by our behavior? And is that theoretical consideration always more important than actually voting for someone whose policies will likely bless our fellow citizens?

Often, worshiping this religious idol of moral purity is a way of saying that the only thing that matters is my conscience before God. But what if we are mistaken in this, and the state of our conscience is merely a self-serving illusion? What if pride and a desire to appear "respectable" before men is really at the heart of our decision?

Related to these things is something else, which we may call an idol of fatalism. We believe that what we do in this world doesn't matter very much because "God is sovereign." Whatever happens happens, so we shouldn't try too hard to change anything. Our job is to worry about our relationship with God over all else, or perhaps our job is to lead others to God—but that's the extent of what He requires of us. But this attitude is false and unbiblical. God calls us to be salt and light. He calls us to do all we are able to do to bless our fellow men and women, and there is much we can do along such lines.

Many Christians have another view. "If the world around us goes to Hell," they say, "so be it. We are not citizens of this world, and in the end, everything will burn." In other words, what we do isn't likely to change anything, and whether anything changes doesn't ultimately matter. Or perhaps the thinking is that we are already under judgment and deserve to be, and there's nothing we can do about it. It is God's job to tell us when we can sit back and stop fighting for what is right and good and true, but some people have already decided that fighting isn't worth the effort because the outcome has been decided already. That's the openly negative side of this temptation to fatalism.

But the other side of worshiping this idol of fatalism expresses itself in a much sunnier way. Some will see evil arising on all fronts and say, "God is on His throne!" And, of course, He is. No one can dispute that. But what does this mean? Was God not on His throne when Christians countenanced chattel slavery in the United States? Did God being on His throne at that time mean that those who knew slavery was an offense to Him didn't need to work hard on every front to end slavery, including politically? Or didn't they think the issue mattered to God? Was God not on His throne when the Nazis created a system by which they were able to butcher millions of innocent souls? Did that mean those who could do something about it were absolved of doing anything simply because God was on His throne?

We know that ultimately, God's answer to evil is always God Himself; and more specifically than that, we know that His answer to evil is Jesus, whom He sent into the world two thousand years ago. His willingness to die for us, and His subsequent resurrection from the dead, are God's answer to evil. But we cannot forget that He also sent His Holy Spirit down to us so that we could be His answer, in His strength and in His power, to the world's problems while we are here. So we must reject this idol of fatalism as strongly as we reject Satan himself.

To help us see what it might look like for us to really follow Jesus—to practice a genuinely "religionless Christianity" and thereby avoid worshiping the religious idols we have mentioned—we will now look at the final years of Bonhoeffer's life.

CHAPTER NINE

Bonhoeffer Burns His Boats

*I have come to the conclusion that I have made a mistake
in coming to America. I must live through this difficult
period of our national history with the Christian people
of Germany.*

—*Dietrich Bonhoeffer, 1939*

In the summer of 1939, Dietrich Bonhoeffer made a breathtaking decision: He chose to leave the seeming safety of a life in America which his friends had arranged for him and go back to Germany, which was on the verge of war. But how did he make this decision, which to us looks so extraordinarily brave? Or perhaps we think it was somehow foolhardy, since we now know that the Nazis would eventually execute him just before the war's end? How did he live out what he would call "religionless Christianity" at this crucial time?

In a nutshell, the answer to this question is that one must have an actual relationship with God. There is no substitute for this, although there are many "religious" ways in which we imagine we are doing God's will. But they cannot work. To live truly as a Christian and to be genuinely free to do God's will really does require a living relationship with the God of the Bible. Anything else is a cheap religious facsimile which, in the end, results in avoiding God's will. Principles and rules are like training wheels we eventually are obliged to remove so that we can more freely follow God's leading.

But if we really do have this relationship with God and are able to be truly free in following His leading, we will gain strength and courage as we go. It comes automatically and inevitably when we really do know Him and walk with Him. If we have genuine faith, we will experience God giving us courage. If one consults the Scriptures—particularly Revelation 22—one sees that courage is not an extra-credit virtue intended only for a handful of Christian believers. Without faith, the Bible says, it is impossible to please God. And it follows that without the courage that only comes from real faith, it is impossible to live out our Christianity in any real sense. If we actually believe what the Bible says about God, and if we know Him personally, courage miraculously follows. We don't need to work it up. Great faith and courage are also the result of sanctification, which comes as we walk with God in faith and obedience. There is a process involved.

We know that Bonhoeffer followed God's leading from the beginning of the rise of the Nazis all the way to the end of the war and his own death, and we know that along the way, he was often tempted toward merely "religious" answers to what he faced, as any of us are in our walk with God. But he kept his eyes on God when many others didn't.

The Bible didn't have an easy answer to the complex issues Bonhoeffer faced. There was certainly no safe answer. Oftentimes, walking with God requires a measure of daring, of being willing to step out in faith, knowing that we may even be getting things wrong in some ways. Bonhoeffer's way forward with God was, in some respects, the antithesis of what we have called "religious" ways of dealing with things. But let's examine his story, so that we can understand some of the details and better appreciate the whole.

Bonhoeffer made many decisions that we may see as "boat burning" moments throughout his life, but this one in July 1939 stands apart. The background of what happened that summer begins earlier that year. Anyone paying attention could see that Hitler was finally going to bring war to Europe. He had been working toward it for years, but now the moment was finally approaching.

Bonhoeffer was a patriotic German. He was not a pacifist in the sense that we think of that word today, although many have been confused about him on this subject. It is very clear that he did not have any particular objections to picking up a rifle to defend one's country, nor with the general idea of fighting in a "just war." But Bonhoeffer knew that what Hitler was bringing to the world was no "just war," and therefore he could not personally participate in what was coming. He also knew that men born in 1906 would soon be drafted, which would leave him no choice. What to do?

His situation was complicated for several reasons. Because of his influential role in the Confessing Church, Bonhoeffer could not openly declare himself against the war without putting all of his colleagues in danger. It was one thing for him to risk his own life in following God, but he knew he could not insist that everyone else join him. He also knew that many in the Confessing Church would feel that fighting in the war was the right thing.

Nor did Bonhoeffer feel that was the time to make a public statement of where he stood. Although he was not afraid to say whatever must be said when he felt it was the right time to say it, neither was he the sort of person who felt he must always broadcast his thoughts on every matter. Prudence and practicality were real issues for him, as they should be for any of us. Even as late as 1939, Bonhoeffer still believed that he had options open to him in which he could fight against Hitler and the Nazis. But what exactly was God asking of him now? What role did God want him to play going forward?

In the years leading up to 1939, Bonhoeffer was always reacting to the changing situation. What he said and did in 1933 and 1934 was not the same as what he would say in 1936 or 1937. While he was not evolving in his theology—which was essentially fixed, as we have said—he was nonetheless evolving in how he reacted to the changing situation. In 1933 and 1934, he was mostly involved in the struggle to wake up the German church to what he believed their role was in standing against Hitler. But by 1935, he realized that battle was over, and that the German church had not stood against Hitler.

So in 1935, 1936, and 1937, he decided that he must spend most of his time preparing young men for ordination, to prepare a future generation of actual disciples of Christ who were not merely "religious." During this time, he oversaw a seminary northeast of Berlin in Pomerania, called Finkenwalde, and he continued to write. But the Nazis tightened their grip on Germany and on the German church every day, and eventually they shut down this seminary. Nonetheless, Bonhoeffer cleverly found a way to continue to teach these young men through an underground seminary. But after a while, this too became impossible. Eventually the Nazis forbade Bonhoeffer from speaking publicly. And finally, they forbade him from writing—or actually from publishing his writings, since he continued to write even into the last weeks of his life in 1945.

Bonhoeffer continued to ask God what to do under the constantly changing circumstances, and then he did what he felt God wanted him to do. He was always feeling his way forward as best he could in that regard.

But in 1939 he came to a genuine impasse. How could he avoid fighting in a war in which his conscience would not allow him to fight without endangering the lives of his colleagues in the Confessing Church?

This was when his American friends intervened. Several of those he had come to know in 1930 and 1931 had stayed in touch with him and understood that his life was now in serious danger. They knew he would almost certainly be sent to a concentration camp, where he would likely lose his life, as friends of his already had. So these American friends came up with a solution: they would invite him to teach and lecture in the United States for an extended period. When the war broke out, he would already be safely away from Germany. Furthermore, he would avoid having to make some dramatic declaration about his feelings on Hitler and the war. He could therefore allow his brethren in the Confessing Church to follow their own consciences, which in many cases meant that they would allow themselves to be drafted into the German military.

Bonhoeffer's closest friends strongly urged him to take the Americans up on this offer. It seemed to be God's wonderful answer to the problem. And so on June 4, 1939, Bonhoeffer boarded a ship to sail across the Atlantic, planning to remain in the United States for two or three years—or indefinitely, depending on what happened in Germany.

But no sooner was he aboard the ship than his conscience—or what he surmised was his conscience—began to bother him. Whatever it was, it seemed as though some preternatural force was pulling him backward to Germany. This is where spiritual maturity and discernment come into play. Was this God speaking to him, or simply some sense of religious guilt? Or was it the voice of the devil? How do we ever know such things for sure? That is part of the larger question in answering what it means to follow God and in practicing "religionless Christianity" rather than mere "religion" or "religiosity." There are a host of easy "religious" answers that many people are all too happy to provide. But the real question is always: What is God Himself saying?

Bonhoeffer couldn't say for sure why he felt as he did, but when he debarked in New York on June 12, the feeling did not go away, but became more urgent. So his initial plans to stay two or three years very quickly changed. Within a few days of his arrival, he had decided that he would stay a year at the most. He felt that he must go back to continue his work in Germany. But a few days later, his feelings toward returning grew stronger still, and he felt that he must go back far sooner—probably in only a few months.

How would he know what was right? In a word, there was no right answer to be found. This did not mean that Bonhoeffer was not consulting the Scriptures, but he knew that they nowhere contained information that would make it clear whether remaining in Germany or leaving for America was the right answer. Nonetheless, he read the Scriptures daily, as he always did, wanting God to speak to him *through them*. Reading his diary from this period makes clear how torturous the whole process was for him. When he is on the verge of deciding to go back very soon, he writes:

> Of course I still keep having second thoughts about my decision. One could have also given quite different reasons.... And is this almost incomprehensible and hitherto almost completely unknown homesickness an accompanying sign from above to make refusal easier for me?...Will I regret it? I may not...I don't know where I am. But he knows, and in the end all doings and actions will be pure and clear.[1]

Again, there is no substitute for a living relationship with God. The Bible was hardly going to provide a clear answer to Bonhoeffer's personal question. He hoped to hear from God himself through the Scriptures, but how exactly? Bonhoeffer wasn't sure. He was wondering if the unprecedented feelings of homesickness were a sign from God, designed to help him choose to return. So obviously Bonhoeffer believed that God spoke through signs and via means other than the Bible, although of course God would never contradict what He said in the Bible.

Bonhoeffer was wrestling with God, praying and trying to find God's will as best he could. But sometimes things are still unclear, and we must simply do the best we can. We must cast our cares and decisions upon God, asking Him to continue to lead us because we really can trust Him. So perhaps—as with Bonhoeffer in this case—we make a decision without knowing for sure whether we are right, but we trust God will guide us. We know He doesn't want us paralyzed in inaction while we wait for an unmistakable answer. Bonhoeffer knew it is wrong to hide in the false safety of doing nothing, of remaining "neutral." And yet that is often precisely the "religious" answer to such difficulties as he faced. Bonhoeffer had seen so many in the German church—and even his colleagues in the Confessing Church—opt for the false security of doing nothing. Of dithering. Of waiting. As though God were not an encouraging father, but rather a dour, judgmental, "religious" God waiting for us to make the wrong move so that He might condemn us. As though doing nothing were the safest option.

Although the phrase likely did not originate with Bonhoeffer, it nonetheless sums up this thinking so well that we often associate it with him: "Silence in the face of evil is itself evil. Not to speak is to speak. Not to act is to act. God will not hold us guiltless." Doing nothing is rarely the option God calls us to choose. The idea that "remaining neutral" is always the safe option is a particularly "religious" and diabolical lie. It has often worked very effectively in deceiving Christians. It is related to worshiping the "idol of purity" we have mentioned. Bonhoeffer knew that doing nothing at this time was not the answer. He must choose and must act, and would trust God as he did so.

And that is what he did. Twenty-six days after Bonhoeffer arrived in New York, he boarded a ship and headed back across the Atlantic. It was a daring, heroic, and extraordinary decision. It is sometimes easy to talk about trusting God, but we can see that Bonhoeffer was doing it quite radically. He really had put his life in God's hands. Many begged him not to do it and gave innumerable "reasonable," "Christian," and "religious" reasons for staying in the United States. But because he sensed God leading him back to Germany, Bonhoeffer feared doing the safe and cautious thing of staying in America far more than he feared returning.

He was a man of genuine faith. Because he really did believe God was leading him back, he did not hesitate to do so. For him, the idea that our lives are in God's hands and "God is in control" was not some pious fiction. He knew it was true, and he proved that he knew it by doing what he did. He knew that unless one puts one's faith into real action, it is no faith at all.

The American theologian Reinhold Niebuhr was one of those who had pulled strings to enable Bonhoeffer to come to America. So Bonhoeffer wrote to him to explain his decision:

> I had had the time to think and to pray about my situation and that of my nation and to have God's will for me clarified. I have come to the conclusion that I have made a

mistake in coming to America. I must live through this difficult period of our national history with the Christian people of Germany. I shall have no right to participate in the reconstruction of Christian life in Germany after the war if I do not share the trials of this time with my people. My brothers in the Confessing [Church] wanted me to go. They may have been right in urging me to do so, but I was wrong in going. Such a decision each man must make for himself. Christians in Germany will face the terrible alternative of either willing the defeat of their nation in order that Christian civilization may survive or willing the victory of their nation and thereby destroying our civilization. I know which of the alternatives I must choose, but I cannot make that choice in security.[2]

Bonhoeffer's return to Germany in July 1939 was an extraordinary act of faith in a life filled with them. Just as Alexander's forces had burned their boats, Bonhoeffer made a retreat to safety impossible. Indeed, because of the war drums heard around the world at that time, the ship on which he returned to Germany ended up being one of the last ships to travel to that nation. The portcullis was coming down, and Bonhoeffer chose to be on the outside, where he would not be safe in the natural sense, but where he knew he would be in God's hands.

As everyone had been expecting, a month after Bonhoeffer returned to Berlin, the Nazis made their vicious and unprovoked attack on Poland, plunging the world into war. Bonhoeffer did not know what the future held for him at that time. He did not know whether he would live or die. But because he genuinely knew Jesus had defeated death, he knew the only life worth living was one utterly devoted to following God, wherever that would lead. That was real freedom. In *The Cost of Discipleship* he had written, "When Christ calls a man, he bids him come and die."[3] Bonhoeffer knew that death to self was the only way to real life in Christ, and life in Christ was the only real life one could ever live.

Years earlier, Bonhoeffer had preached a sermon about death. "No one has yet believed in God," he said, "and in the kingdom of God...no one has yet heard about the realm of the resurrected, and not been homesick from that hour, waiting and looking forward joyfully to being released from bodily existence.... Death is hell and night and cold, if it is not transformed by our faith. But that is just what is so marvelous, that we can transform death."[4]

If one genuinely believed, one would long for Heaven. It was the only logical response. So the question comes to us. Do we really believe in that way, so that we are truly free? Or have we allowed the secular culture to tempt us to a cheap "religious" counterfeit of such faith?

Bonhoeffer obviously had come not merely to hope that God was real and the Bible true, but to know those things utterly. So in 1939 and later, when he faced death, he genuinely knew that there was nothing to fear. It was not any mere pretense of courage. That fearlessness is what constitutes real faith, not merely "religious" faith, and it was what enabled Bonhoeffer to live in genuine freedom and to be joyfully obedient to God's will—even until the very end.

CHAPTER TEN

Mere "Religion" vs. Following God

In returning to Germany in the summer of 1939, Bonhoeffer had made what for him was the ultimate decision. It is a testament to his tremendous faith and to his courage. But then came an important question. Now that he was back, what precisely would he do? The answer is astonishing. What he would do now would require him to trust God and follow His leading in a way he really never had before. And in doing so, he would have to confront a number of "religious" objections and some of the religious idols we have already mentioned.

Once more, we need the background of what he was facing to understand what he did. Did he still believe God wanted him to avoid serving in the military? If so, how would he do that, now that he was no longer in America? And if he wasn't going to fight in the war, what exactly did he plan to do instead? At first he thought he might apply to be a military chaplain, but that door was soon shut. Then what?

What he did next was so extraordinary that many Christians today still have "religious" objections to it, feeling that he betrayed some core Christian principles: He allowed his brother-in-law, Hans von Dohnanyi, to recruit him to serve in Germany's military intelligence service. It is hard to overstate what a dramatic decision this was. In doing this, he "officially" joined the German war effort as a spy. But unofficially, he was precisely the opposite: this pastor and theologian was a double agent, directly involved in the conspiracy to assassinate Adolf Hitler.

We must explain that Germany's military intelligence—called the Abwehr—was the center of the conspiracy against Hitler, and had been for several years. While the Gestapo, the SS, and other parts of the Third Reich were obviously dedicated to serving Hitler's wishes, the Abwehr was something else entirely. Of course, it was "officially" pro-Hitler. What other options were there in a totalitarian state? But within the Abwehr were several figures who deeply opposed Hitler and who formed the center of the conspiracy against him. The Abwehr had been involved in this since the early 1930s, and Bonhoeffer's brother-in-law was one of its principal leaders.

The Nazi leadership assumed that with the nation at war, everyone would do what they must, including the formerly difficult Pastor Bonhoeffer. It appeared he had finally understood the inevitable situation and had somehow made his peace with it. Besides, what Bonhoeffer could do for the Abwehr made logical sense: because of his work with church leaders around Europe over the years, he had many connections. So the Abwehr said that Bonhoeffer would use these international connections to help them and Germany. Bonhoeffer would be a great asset in this capacity, far more than he would be by simply serving in the German army.

But in reality, Bonhoeffer would be using his new position in the Abwehr as a cover for what he was really doing: helping them in the conspiracy against Adolf Hitler. Bonhoeffer had been doing this in an unofficial capacity over the years. Many in his family were involved in the conspiracy and he had been present at many of their meetings in his home, so he was familiar with the territory. But as a theologian and pastor, he had always been somewhat on the outside, providing moral support and spiritual guidance. But now he would fully and officially immerse himself in this conspiracy and in all of the deception that entailed. And that brings up many ethical and moral—and "religious"—questions.

In negotiating his way through these concerns, Bonhoeffer was obliged to avoid simplistic "religious" answers and actually try to discern where God was leading him. This is the heart of the answer to how we avoid the pitfalls of being merely "religious." If we are genuinely following Jesus, we cannot go wrong. But if we substitute "religious" thinking—legalistic and "safe" answers or simply following religious rules—we will inevitably go astray. Doing the "religious" thing will look good to those who think along "religious" lines, and doing what God requires of us may rub these same people the wrong way, just as Jesus did with the religious leaders who eventually killed him. But our obligation is to do God's will, not succumb to what the Bible calls a "fear of man," even—and perhaps especially—if those men are "respected" religious leaders.

So what were the issues confronting Bonhoeffer?

Perhaps the first issue was simply the question of whether it was permissible for a Christian to participate in a deep conspiracy of deception. Wasn't joining the Abwehr essentially to be living a lie? And wasn't lying clearly prohibited for those who called themselves Christians? What could be clearer than that commandment? If this was true, wouldn't the more traditional Christian response be for Bonhoeffer simply to face facts and accept that he must really join the war effort, in earnest, as many of his friends and fellow pastors were doing? Or if he really did believe that doing so violated his conscience and God's will, wouldn't it be better if he simply refused to fight, even though it would likely mean being sent to a concentration camp where he would likely die? How could this very complicated effort to deceive others be God's will?

Again, we should be clear that his thinking in all of this was not merely to find some clever way through a tangled mess. At the heart of it all was the question: *What would God have me do? What do the Scriptures say about these things?*

The second question Bonhoeffer had to answer was whether it was permissible for a Christian to be involved in a plot to kill a human being, even if that human being was Adolf Hitler. There was no doubt that was the principal goal of the conspiracy he had now officially entered. Was that not simply murder? The question was obviously gravely serious.

Thirdly, Bonhoeffer had to deal with the scriptural injunction that we are to avoid the "appearance of evil." Surely his joining the Abwehr would look to many inside and outside the church as though he had finally acceded to the Nazis and was now working for them—the epitome of the appearance of evil. What impact would that have on those who had always looked up to him as a brave leader in the fight against Hitler and all he represented?

Finally, Bonhoeffer had to answer the overarching question of whether he ought to simply give up and accept the grim options left to him. Hadn't he perhaps come to the end of his battles, and hadn't he been faithful to God? What more could he do? Why was it necessary to do something as dramatic as joining non-Christians in a conspiracy to assassinate the head of the nation? Could that really be God's will? How could God be calling one of His servants to dirty his hands in this way? Wasn't it more honorable to nobly accept defeat? Or to have stayed in America, where everyone had urged him to stay?

Let's address this fourth question first. Did God really want Bonhoeffer to continue fighting against the Nazis at that juncture? The nation was at war, and the church had failed to stand up to the Nazis when it had the chance. Wasn't the battle over for Bonhoeffer? Hadn't he done all he could?

Bonhoeffer didn't believe so, mainly because he felt a moral obligation toward the victims of the Nazis. Principally, this meant the Jews, but there were many others, too, who would suffer if good men like Dietrich Bonhoeffer threw in the towel at that juncture. So while many might have been tempted to give up—and would have been applauded for doing so—he simply felt that he could not. He had written of the Christians' obligations to the Jews back in 1933, and he knew now that he might well be able to do something.

Yes, he might have stayed in the United States in order to survive to do more in the future. Or he might have come back to Germany and persuaded himself that, as per Romans 13, he had an obligation to fight for his country, however much he didn't like the idea. Or he might have flatly refused to fight and gone to a concentration camp. Each of these options was open to him, but all three essentially would have been the end of his fighting against the Nazis. Bonhoeffer believed that if he could still do something to help defeat the Nazis and Hitler, he must do it.

Not to continue fighting in some way—if there were some way that he could continue—would be to bow to several of the religious idols we have mentioned. One would be the religious idol of fatalism, as though to say the battle was over even if it wasn't. It also would have involved bowing to the religious idols of respectability and purity: Bonhoeffer would really be thinking more about the state of his soul—in a pietistic, solipsistic, detached, and selfish way—than about the millions who would be affected by what he did or didn't do if he chose that route.

So let's go back to the first question concerning whether deception is permissible for a Christian. It is one thing to say, "I won't fight," and to suffer the consequences. It is another to say, "I will indeed join the German war effort," only to actually be working against the German war effort. Was that not simply lying and bearing false witness?

Bonhoeffer had thought of this quite a bit over the years. He did not have a simplistic or legalistic view of whether "lying" was permissible. He would, of course, have been familiar with the story of Rahab in the Old Testament book of Joshua, and from that could deduce that there is sometimes a greater principle at play—and at that point, doing the easy "religious" thing and simply saying, "I cannot tell a lie" would be morally wrong. Bonhoeffer knew that millions of lives were at stake in his choice. Would God not hold him responsible for what happened if he didn't do whatever he could? He knew that God would, and that falling upon "religious" objections to deception in the face of the towering evils of the Third Reich would really be a combination of cowardice and fear.

Also, when it came to the evil figures who led the Third Reich, Bonhoeffer didn't feel that he "owed them the truth," as he termed it. In his book *Ethics*, Bonhoeffer writes about this concept. He asks us to suppose a teacher asks a girl in front of the class whether her father is an alcoholic. Bonhoeffer argues that that girl does not owe the teacher the truth. To dishonor her father in that way would be worse than telling the "truth" of the matter. So simply to answer "no" would not fall under the category of lying or bearing false witness in the way the Bible puts it, because the Bible also enjoins us to honor our father and our mother. We have also mentioned the scenario in which the Gestapo asks us if we are hiding a Jew. Bonhoeffer knew that "telling the truth" under such circumstances would be a cynical deception and a legalistic dodge. To turn the Jew over is to have a distorted view of God—seeing Him not as a loving Father who calls us to do right out of love for Him and our fellow man, but as a dour moral policeman who only wants to catch us doing something wrong.

So the "religious" temptation to appear morally pure while actually throwing the fate of other human beings aside was something Bonhoeffer took very seriously. He had not always been entirely settled on the answer. Indeed, it was his sister-in-law, Emmi Bonhoeffer—married to his brother Klaus—who helped clarify this question for him. Neither were Christians, but both were deeply involved in the plot against Hitler, as many in the family were, though Bonhoeffer himself had avoided it while he struggled to get the German church to speak out and take action. He knew what his family and others were involved in meant potentially killing Hitler. But at some point, his sister-in-law called him out. "You Christians are glad when someone else does what you know must be done," she said, "but it seems that somehow you are unwilling to get your own hands dirty and do it."[1]

Surely this must have stung Bonhoeffer. Was it true? It was perhaps this comment that pushed him to think more deeply about these issues and finally to decide that he must indeed "get his hands dirty" with the others who were doing so. Was it morally acceptable for him to hang back as a Christian while others did what he wouldn't? He didn't think so. But several things must be said so that we may understand his thinking.

First of all, there was no question he had qualms about the plot to kill Hitler. We know that he spoke about it with some of his close friends as he tried to make sense of it from a moral standpoint. But in the end, he knew that it was not murder, which God clearly prohibits. We know that David killed Goliath, and we hardly call that murder. We know that many figures in the Bible were involved in military efforts in which people were killed, but we don't think of those killings as murders. Bonhoeffer, in one conversation, used the analogy of someone driving a car down a busy street, killing people left and right as he ran them over. Would a policeman or anyone else not have a moral obligation to shoot that driver, knowing that lives would be saved? Of course that would not be thought of as murder.

That's how Bonhoeffer saw the situation with Hitler. He and those in the conspiracy had no doubt that Hitler was in fact murdering millions. It wasn't a question of whether God would forgive them if they took action to stop him, even if that meant killing him. It was rather a question of whether God would forgive them if they did nothing.

Bonhoeffer said clearly many times that to live out one's faith meant not to hang back in fear of making some mistake, but to dare to act—knowing that inaction caused by fear of making a mistake is the real sin.

The religious idols of purity and respectability we have mentioned are obviously temptations in this calculation, and caused many German Christians to do nothing when they might have done something, thinking this was the safe "religious" response. But we know the unspeakable horror that resulted from that stance. They thought they would remain on the fence and be somehow "neutral"; they were unaware that the devil himself owned the fence and was pleased to have them sit on it. Their "religious" understanding of the situation suited his purposes perfectly, just as the false "religious" thinking of many Christians in our own time does.

The idol of respectability also tempted Bonhoeffer in another sense: He knew joining the German military intelligence unit would be misunderstood by many whose opinion mattered to him. Although he believed he was following God in what he was doing, it was something he could not discuss much, even with friends. It was a covert operation, and to speak of it to the wrong person would not merely endanger his own life but those of everyone involved. Despite knowing that many would disapprove of his decision, he could not go to them and explain himself. It was a real example of "death to self."

Here was a dramatic example of not being pulled away from God's will by the stern disapproval of others, including those whom we might deeply respect. At the top of this list was the towering figure of Karl Barth, whom Bonhoeffer had admired since he began studying theology many years before. Barth in turn thought as highly of Bonhoeffer as anyone, and had in 1927 declared the twenty-one-year-old genius's dissertation a "theological miracle." After this, they came to know each other, so that Barth was something of a fatherly influence.

But the relationship went far beyond mere theological agreement: Barth had been among the staunchest figures in the theological world to stand against the Nazis. He had essentially written the Barmen Declaration himself—and had personally mailed a copy of it to Adolf Hitler. No one had been more heroic in confronting the Nazis' aggressively anti-church actions, and because of this, the Nazis had deported Barth to Switzerland in 1935, where he was now teaching at the University of Basel. Bonhoeffer knew that once the war began, Barth and others would wonder what in the world he was doing. It didn't look good.

Indeed, from all outward appearances, Bonhoeffer now had an impossibly charmed life. Why was he not facing death on the front lines of the war or in a concentration camp as so many others in the Confessing Church now were? He was free to travel around Germany, to attend operas and films, and did so. What must this have looked like to those who had known him as a prophetic and serious voice of courage? He even traveled to Switzerland and Sweden. How had he escaped the grim fate of the rest of his generation? Had he himself gone over to the dark side or struck some compromise with the forces of darkness?

The situation with his friend Barth actually came to a head in February 1941 when the Abwehr sent Bonhoeffer to Switzerland. His obviously dangerous and secret mission was to make contact with church leaders outside Germany to let them know about those within the Abwehr conspiring against Hitler. But for some reason, the Swiss border police wouldn't let Bonhoeffer into the country until someone in Switzerland vouched for him. Not knowing what else to do, Bonhoeffer named Barth. Barth did vouch for Bonhoeffer, but not without some serious misgivings. What Barth thought, we cannot know. But we know it must have been difficult for Bonhoeffer to be unable to explain himself to someone whose approval he surely must have longed for, and now could not have.[2]

All of this illustrates the idea that in the end, we answer for our actions to God. We may wish to avoid any "appearance of evil," but sometimes looking respectable is something we are obliged to forego for God's purposes. No one more than Jesus Himself lived this out. In fulfilling the very mission for which His Father had sent him to our broken and sin-sick planet, He was forced to bear the ultimate indignity of crucifixion, to be mocked and misunderstood. But He endured it because He cared more about doing His Father's will than about being praised by men.

CHAPTER ELEVEN

Are We Approaching the End of Time?

As we said at the beginning of this book, we seem to be living at the end of time. That's a dramatically dramatic statement. If there is any truth to it, we must ask what evidence we have to support it. And then we must ask where exactly on the fabled timeline toward the end of time we might be. Are we on the verge of going over the roaring cataract into oblivion, or might we still somehow avert that prophesied disaster for a time? If enough people who call themselves Christians were to wake up now, recognize where we are, and really live out a "religionless Christianity," could we avert what seems to lie immediately ahead? What might God be saying to us now, and what might He want us to do? Is our quickly approaching end simply inevitable, or might we be able to act in such a way as to give ourselves a reprieve? What is God's will for us now?

In any case, there is at least significant evidence to suggest that we shouldn't bat the question away, as though it's simply not possible that the end is nigh. To do that is to fall into the fatal error of secularism, as we have been outlining. The Bible is clear as crystal that history will end, and our discomfort with the idea is no argument against it but only an argument for our own participation in the process of secularization—of which we must repent. These ideas simply cannot be dismissed by anyone daring to identify as a serious Christian. So let us at least consider the evidence at hand to gain some sense of where we stand.

At the top of the list of the evidence for the idea that we are approaching the prophesied end of history is the emergence of national Israel from the proverbial ashes of history in 1948. To any student of history, it is an arresting fact that this happened twenty long centuries after the Roman Empire—with the most extreme brutality—wiped Israel off the face of the map, after which its inhabitants were scattered to the four corners of the globe, where all natural reason would predict they would evaporate into the atmosphere, just as the Hittites and Amorites and Jebusites and other tribes of that era did. Who could have imagined that these people might over the ages somehow retain their identities as Jews? That alone is astonishing, and argues that their identity is utterly unlike that of any other people who have lived on this planet.

When Frederick the Great of Prussia in the eighteenth century was asked for proof of God, he supposedly gave a simple and decisive two-word answer: "The Jews." What else could conceivably account for their continued existence? If the answer is not simply "God," the question must itself be absolutely maddening. Any other answers to the question seem torturously contrived.

But the wildly astonishing existence of the Jews for so long all around the globe, in often tremendously hostile circumstances, and then the more astonishing fact of so many of them reversing the course of that diaspora to return to their place of origin and then forming the modern nation of Israel, is often cited as evidence that we are near the end of history.

Israel's continued existence since 1948—and the dramatic expansion of her borders since then—must be regarded as equally astounding, if not simply miraculous, given the formidable and dedicatedly hostile powers arrayed against her during all these decades. And those forces have never been more hostile or powerful than they are today. Anyone with a mind even slightly open to the idea of a God of history must realize how powerfully these things argue that we are palpably nearing the end of that timeline.

On the other hand, we have been living with modern Israel for three-quarters of a century, such that many who have grudgingly marveled at the idea over the decades might by now have begun to shrug at it. What of it? There is much to be said on the topic and much that has already been said, so let's put it aside to consider something else that has emerged more recently that is at least equally astonishing and that must lead us to consider seriously whether we are living near the end of time.

One World Government

Among those things anyone conversant on the topic of the End Times must consider *de rigueur* is the idea of a one-world government. We must know that such a regime will not resemble anything like the one the American Founders created 250 years ago. But many of us are shocked to see the increasing plausibility of such a thing in the near term. Obviously we are not quite there yet, but quite suddenly, several trends and forces have begun aligning toward the reality of this madness. The extraordinary speed of it obliges us at least to wonder what might be happening, because most of us could not until very recently have begun to imagine how it might take shape. But suddenly we have some ideas how it could—which is more than a little horrifying.

When two or more decades ago such now-marginalized figures as Alex Jones—always stridently denounced as an irresponsible "conspiracy theorist"—would speak of such things, it was wonderfully easy to laugh and sneer. Back then, the idea of what he called "open borders" and a "cashless society" sounded too far-fetched to take at all seriously. How could such things ever happen? The idea of an oligarchy of "globalist elites" pushing such ideas and using the excuses of "public health emergencies" to take away our fundamental rights as Americans also seemed like perfect madness. That such "globalist elites" actually existed, and that they would publicly say there are too many people on the planet and that we need to "cull" the human population—which must translate to mass murder on a scale that would make Mao, Stalin, and Hitler himself blush in embarrassment— seemed nothing but the sheerest insanity to almost anyone except those who dared to wallow outside what were once thought "respectable" circles.

And yet, here we are.

Is it now not we ourselves who preened to live within those "respectable" circles who should blush for dismissing these things, and especially for doing so with such tremendous high-handedness and self-satisfaction as we did? Is it not almost too much to bear to think that we could be that wrong, and that we could be that cockily self-assured of our rightness? Because—*mirabile dictu*—all of these things prophesied by those we excoriated and damned as hucksters and conspiracy theorists have suddenly arrived, just as these figures said to anyone who would listen despite the howls of derision they faced. Are we now not at least embarrassed, and even ashamed? How could we have been so willfully blind to the possibilities?

Many of us have now and again wondered over the decades what the antichrist system prophesied in Scripture might look like if it came into being in our lifetimes. Some were influenced by such books as Hal Lindsey's *The Late Great Planet Earth*, or perhaps by David Wilkerson's *The Vision*. But what these men and others described in the 1970s seemed so extreme and implausible that, as easy as it was for us to be terrified by their thoughts, it was even easier to dismiss them as febrile hysteria. At that time, cell phones and the internet were more than twenty-five years in the future. We were in a Cold War with the Soviet Union. And yet, as with the prophecies of secular seers such as Alex Jones, the seemingly outlandish visions sketched out for us by those such as Lindsey and Wilkerson have rather recently and very quickly become stunningly plausible, if not outright actualities.

To quote the cliché, the unthinkable has suddenly become thinkable. What a moment ago seemed a fever dream is now the news of the day. The utter moral breakdown that people like Wilkerson prophesied seemed so far beyond our ken that it was impossible to do anything but ignore it at the time. Nonetheless, as we know today, men dressed as women writhe with sexual suggestiveness in public, sometimes on parade floats with children watching, and sometimes at much closer quarters. More than that, their apologists insist that everyone must celebrate these nightmares as a logical extension of those liberties that began with our Founding and continued with the abolition of slavery and the suffragist and civil rights movements. If this weren't the furthest extreme of madness, parents wishing to seem "progressive" have successfully been persuaded into thinking it the height of open-mindedness to subject their innocent young children to these disturbing spectacles.

The idea seems to be that we must all become dulled to the natural repulsion we feel toward such things as part of our "reeducation" toward something. But what? What plausible future can such things portend? In any case, anything once thought wholesome or normal or normative or good or laudable must now be spat upon as despicable. Many of the confused and broken human beings involved in these public behaviors often seem to go to considerable lengths to ally themselves with the openly demonic, as though to inure everyone not merely to the sexual confusion but to the demonic itself. But who has decided that we are all to gallop along in this Gadarene mob?

Of course, much of our own government and even our military have bowed to these idols. Corporate America has cravenly joined this chorus, waving their increasingly and perplexingly complex "pride" flags with far greater enthusiasm than any patriot ever waved the Stars and Stripes. The most predictably "transgressive" brands, such as Balenciaga, have employed openly satanic designers for whom the aggressively wicked sexualization of children has obviously been intentional, with little blowback from the high-end sophisticates who shop there (or wish they could) and for whom nothing can ever be shocking. But even so-called mainstream retailers such as Target have gone along with this evil, pushing transgender ideology in their children's departments and even hiring designers who are unapologetically pushing explicitly satanic images. Brands that were once the most "American" and mainstream—such as Disney and Anheuser-Busch—have done precisely the same. It seems almost impossible that these things can be true, and yet they are well documented for anyone not yet convinced. No sane person could imagine these things actually happening even a few years ago, and of course those pushing against them by standing up for the most basic ideas such as the importance of the normative family and protecting the innocence of children are themselves demonized as cruel and censorious bigots, or labeled with any term that might suffice to do the job of demonizing anyone who sees these things for what they are—which is at least child abuse and insanity, and likely openly demonic too, as we have said.

The most basic concepts of our lives for centuries and sometimes for millennia are now challenged as not merely outmoded, but as inherently vile. The fundamental and deeply sensible idea of national borders is suddenly cast as "nationalistic," as though Adolf Hitler's racist views once and for all made national pride—and borders and patriotism—the vilest things imaginable. We behave as though what was once the healthy love of one's country can only exist as the grotesque caricatured version of it. And naturally into this vacuum—as though on cue—"globalism" is shoved forward as the only answer. Instead of sanely accepting George Washington and Abraham Lincoln's views on patriotism, we are told we must choose either Adolf Hitler's views or reject national patriotism altogether. And what's worse is that many in churches and church leadership are silent in the face of this because they are unwilling to be labeled with the pejorative term "Christian nationalist."

It seems that all of the most radically leftist Marxist ideologies that for decades have bided their time in the shadows of the academy have now suddenly leapt out into the mainstream. They are telling us—shouting at us!—that our children do not belong to us but to the state, that children are sexual beings and innocence does not exist. They are telling us that the most non-racist human beings are racists nonetheless, simply because of the color of their skin—and that they must therefore somehow be punished for the color of their skin. They have insisted that national borders are not a healthy and prudent notion but simply an excuse to keep our country racially pure, just as Hitler wished to do.

It doesn't take a person of any real faith to see genuine evil in all these developments. Indeed, increasing numbers of people who have never been churchgoers or Bible readers have begun to say that these things are evil. For what they are witnessing, they have no other categories to which they might repair. And if these things are worth calling "evil," then the only solution can be God. Many of these formerly agnostic or secular people are, for the first time in their lives, open to the idea of God, and for the first time in many of their lives actually hoping that He does exist. The horrors all around us are a powerful opportunity for evangelism . . . unless you are going to a church that—like many German churches in the 1930s—has its head in the sand and refuses to acknowledge these things and speak boldly against them.

Unfortunately, many do, and have made peace with this devilish madness. Worse still, many churches are actually going further than mere silence by aiding and abetting these false ideologies in deconstructing what ten minutes ago was the reality in which we all lived. Such churches have festooned their facilities with rainbow banners and BLM flags with the same alacrity and fear that many churches in the 1930s hung swastika flags—seeming to have no real idea what these things could mean but only wishing to keep the angry hordes from targeting them, as though this were a genuinely Christian effort at peacemaking rather than the capitulation to evil that it is.

One World Religion

Among the further developments that many such as David Wilkerson have prophesied over the decades is the emergence of not merely a one-world government, but of a global religion. This, too, always sounded impossibly far-fetched, or at least like something that might happen far in the future. And yet we can now see the outlines of this very thing forming all around us.

Of course, this would require the apostasy of many Christian churches. But of all things, that is the easiest to see and has been happening for the longest time already. The lurch leftward to accommodate secularist ideology has been a part of mainline Protestant churches even since before Bonhoeffer went to New York in 1930, where he saw it with his own eyes. But of late, this dark development has come to American evangelical churches too, with evangelicals deliberately blurring the lines on several foundational issues—usually citing "evangelism" as their ultimate reason for doing so. The willingness of once solidly theologically orthodox institutions to accommodate what we may call "wokeness" is deeply shocking and saddening, with *Christianity Today*—founded by the great Billy Graham—heading backward to Babel, dragging the standard of biblical orthodoxy through the mud of its ignominious retreat. Others such as the Gospel Coalition and even CRU—formerly Campus Crusade for Christ, founded by Bill Bright—are similarly embattled in what looks at this point like a losing fight. Although some in these institutions are still on the right side of things, many are singing another tune entirely. And of course, many once-solid evangelical colleges—most prominently Wheaton College in Chicago—have opened their doors to critical race theory and transgender ideology in a way that must be immensely confusing to anyone who not long ago thought of these schools as bulwarks of truth. Many of these institutions were founded as answers to the aggressive secularism of top American universities. Who would dream that sending one's child to such places today might well result in their losing the faith in which they have been raised?

Equally shocking have been developments in the Roman Catholic Church under the seemingly intentionally confusing leadership of its Marxist-leaning pontiff. Many evangelicals have deep doctrinal differences with their Catholic brethren but have always known them to be the staunchest advocates of the unborn and of a Christian sexual ethic. But under increasingly liberal Catholic leadership, these things have changed. To wit: I recently beheld on New York City's Park Avenue a very prominent Catholic church displaying a rainbow banner on a rotating electronic billboard. The banner said, "We welcome our LGBTQ brothers and sisters." I would expect to see this on a left-leaning Lutheran or United Methodist church, but in front of a Catholic church? And what could this strange message really mean? The idea that they welcome their "LGBTQ brothers and sisters" at least means that they now consider the alphabet soup of that adjective legitimate, as though this is an important community whom they must explicitly welcome. And it implicitly says that they don't hold whatever views on sexuality those reading the sign might have expected them to. So what else could the sign really mean except that that congregation had now at last openly broken with two thousand years of church history, and was openly and deliberately blurring the line between virtue and vice? But they had done this in a satanically clever way, framing the message in terms of "inclusion" so that no one could exactly say that this represented a clear and dramatic departure from church teaching—and yet everyone could also see that it was indeed a clear and dramatic departure from church teaching.

Two years ago, I was similarly horrified to see that the Greek Orthodox Church in New York City had agreed to co-celebrate a liturgical service at St. Bartholomew's Episcopal Church on Park Avenue. As someone raised in the Greek Orthodox Church, I was astonished beyond description. Eastern Orthodoxy has often been a world unto itself—both for good and ill—immune to the siren song of Christian ecumenism, which usually means progressivism and modernism. Like the Catholic Church, they had never gone in for the progressive madness of the mainline Protestant churches. To appreciate the shock of what this co-celebration meant, one must know that St. Bartholomew's—or St. Bart's, as it is popularly called—has long been at the forefront of "gay rights," and during the very month in which the Greek Orthodox priests entered this church, it proudly displayed a huge gay-pride banner for all on Park Avenue to see. How had the Greek Orthodox Church come to such a place that it would allow its priests to prostrate themselves—and the historic church and its millions of adherents—to the zeitgeist of sexual confusion by entering this building and "co-celebrating" a religious service with people who for decades had been proudly heretical on this most central of issues? At what point would the leaders of the Greek Orthodox Church in America do something similar in a mosque or a Buddhist Temple? And wasn't the idea behind this their way of doing what the Roman Catholics were doing in displaying their rainbow banner? They were helping normalize the idea that biblical orthodoxy and theology are no longer considered sacred and immutable, but are now changing to the satanic spirit of the age. Like their Catholic brothers and sisters thirty blocks north, they were signaling that they were taking their first steps away from what they had always taught and believed—away from the Orthodox faith for which millions had been martyred in places like Turkey and Armenia and the former Soviet Union.

Isn't this sort of "ecumenism" in the direction of no real belief exactly what a "one-world religion" would look like, were such a thing to emerge? And wouldn't that ecumenism be given over to the spirit of the age, whatever that was? And must that not stand in clear opposition to the historic Christian faith? A "global" faith along these lines would of course put itself forward as more "inclusive" and less "dogmatic" and "authoritarian" than the biblical Christian faith. Of course, it would be none of these things, but precisely their opposites. It would demand everyone's worship and brazenly subvert the doctrines of biblical sexuality in the name of "unity" and "inclusion." One might say that it would cry "Peace! Peace!" But there would be no peace. Is that not what we see emerging, and emerging quickly?

In 2001, after the terrorist strikes of 9/11, Oprah Winfrey and others gathered in Yankee Stadium for a blandly ecumenical service that most serious Christians denounced as New Age and theologically confusing—and therefore, meaningless at best or deliberately and wickedly confusing at worst. Certainly it was of no help to anyone actually looking for God amidst the pain of that tragic time. But who would think that twenty years later, many in the camps of those who had denounced that event would be in league with far more grotesque versions of ecumenism—standing in solidarity with those who mock the biblical views of sexuality and themselves turning backward to a chilling form of pansexual paganism?

What can such things portend?

CHAPTER TWELVE

Resurrecting the Tower of Babel

Then they said, "Come, let us build ourselves a city and a
tower with its top in the heavens, and let us make a name
for ourselves, lest we be dispersed over the face of the
whole earth."

—Genesis 11:4

If it's true that a Last Days globalist movement is indeed taking shape, the question is, what can we do about it? Is it a *fait accompli*, or can the Church of Jesus, by repenting and praying, move God's heart so that He stays the hand of these satanic forces and gives us another chance? Where exactly are we on this prophetic time clock? Are the myriad horrors we are seeing now God's gift to wake us up so that we might do what the German churches did not? Are these sudden ghastly developments His way of saying, "This is only the beginning of what will happen when I withdraw My blessing and favor from you," precisely in order for us to see things clearly—and to repent? And *will* we see these things and repent?

To answer these questions, we return again to the story of the Tower of Babel, which we have said is a picture of "religion" in the negative sense. It is a picture of mankind attempting to ascend into the heavens apart from God. It is also a picture of all the utopianism ideologies that have tried—and failed—to do this, usually murdering millions in the process. In each of these cases throughout history, we were following the siren song of Satan himself, because as we have said, we first hear the invitation to this when Satan tells Eve that she must liberate herself from God and disobey His command if she is to be truly free. This is at the heart of all these efforts. Satan promises us precisely what he wants for himself, which is to usurp the role of God.

By way of background, we remember that before Satan himself "fell" and became the leader of all the rebellious angels who fell with him—whom we now call "demons"—he was an anointed cherub who dwelt in the presence of God. In Ezekiel 28, we read:

> "You were the signet of perfection,
> full of wisdom and perfect in beauty.
> You were in Eden, the garden of God;
> every precious stone was your covering,
> sardius, topaz, and diamond,
> beryl, onyx, and jasper,
> sapphire, emerald, and carbuncle;
> and crafted in gold were your settings
> and your engravings.
> On the day that you were created
> they were prepared.
> You were an anointed guardian cherub.
> I placed you; you were on the holy mountain of God;
> in the midst of the stones of fire you walked.
> You were blameless in your ways
> from the day you were created,
> till unrighteousness was found in you." (vv. 12–15)

Then in the book of Isaiah, we get more information:

> "How you are fallen from heaven,
> O Day Star, son of Dawn!
> How you are cut down to the ground,
> you who laid the nations low!
> You said in your heart,
> 'I will ascend to heaven;
> above the stars of God
> I will set my throne on high;
> I will sit on the mount of assembly
> in the far reaches of the north;
> I will ascend above the heights of the clouds;
> I will make myself like the Most High.'
> But you are brought down to Sheol,
> to the far reaches of the pit." (Isaiah 14:12–15)

The general outlines of the story are that Satan rebelled against God and was cast out of Heaven forever. He who was the "morning star"—sometimes called the "light bearer" or "Lucifer"—was filled with such pride that he succumbed to the temptation to ascend into Heaven and take God's place. This is "religion" as we are defining it (and as Bonhoeffer defined it). It is not merely that we do not worship God and give Him his due, but that we wish ourselves to become God—although we may be the last to see this is what is at play. Either we side with God utterly, or we have sided with the one who wishes to murder God and take His place—in which case we have let Satan enlist us in his rebellion against God. We first fell for this lie when we rebelled against God in Eden, and we fall for it again and again whenever we try to subvert God's plans for us by achieving on our own strength Heaven or utopia or whatever paradise we imagine.

We see echoes of these stories in the ancient Greek myth of Prometheus, who climbed Mount Olympus and stole fire from the gods. Prometheus is often credited with bringing knowledge and technology to mankind and giving them the ability to create civilization. Therefore, his rebellion against the gods of Olympus is seen as a good thing. In the Greek myth, the gods are clearly characterized as being selfishly against human beings—as opposed to the God of the Bible, Who is unequivocally for us and genuinely trying to protect us from ourselves. Of course, many people in our own time see Adam and Eve's transgression not as sinful and harmful, but as something like Prometheus's theft of fire. They see it as liberating—precisely as Satan promised it would be. We can even see a dramatically more harmless echo of this in the innocent childhood fairytale of nimble Jack climbing the skyscraping beanstalk into that realm above the clouds and killing the giant who lives there.

But the biblical version of these tales is that God prohibited us from eating of the Tree of the Knowledge of Good and Evil precisely because He loves us and knew that we would be fatally harmed if we ate of it—which we were indeed. He knew that when we did what He had forbidden, there would be terrible repercussions for us. The point is that we brought these consequences on ourselves—God does not exile us from the Garden out of pique, but out of mercy. And once we left Eden, He began the process of leading us toward His redemptive solution to our fallen state—a plan which was already in place even before He created the world, because He stands outside of time and knew what we would choose. Similarly, when God thwarted the efforts of those who made the Tower of Babel, He did so for their own good. He knew what mankind is capable of apart from Him, and He mercifully prevented us from achieving it at that time. His plan for us is infinitely better than our plan for ourselves. And our plan for ourselves—to achieve paradise apart from Him—is, of course, actually Satan's plan for us.

The story of the Tower of Babel is, in a way, a reprisal of the story of Eden. But the story of the Tower of Babel speaks to us right now in an especially chilling way, precisely because never before in the millennia since it took place have we had the ability to do it again—to come together as a united force of mankind against God. But now we do.

God thwarted mankind's efforts by causing those building the Tower of Babel to speak in many languages. The consolidated power they had before God did this vanished instantly. We know that God in His mercy divided us in this way to prevent us from achieving what was ultimately a satanic project. If we had succeeded back then, we might have precipitated God's final judgment upon us. So we can only assume that God thwarted our efforts so He could execute his own plan to redeem us in the millennia ahead. And of course, we know the story of how He did that: creating for Himself a people out of whom He would bring forth His Messiah, who would die in our place and thereby defeat death and Hell, and open a way for us back to God. Because God thwarted our plans at the Tower of Babel, innumerable millions subsequently have been able to take Him up on His gracious offer to enter Heaven through the sacrifice of Jesus.

We can understand why God thwarted mankind's efforts on that plain in Shinar. He wished to save us from ourselves—and for Himself and His purposes for us. But how He did it is of particular interest: He suddenly caused those working together to speak different languages. We may assume that afterward, those who spoke the same language became a tribe or a nation and found other places to live. In God's doing this, we may observe something like a primitive version of the separation of powers that we find in American government. These people who were suddenly linguistically divided from each other—and scattered by God around the world—were never again united. Our linguistic differences did not merely make it impossible for us to communicate with each other, but divided us along further lines and eventually caused us to oppose each other. And so we have been ever since—at least until very recently.

Right now, several trends and forces are attempting to unite us once again via what we call "globalism." It is hard to avoid the conclusion that Satan is trying once more, in what may well be his final opportunity in human history, and with more vigor than ever, to get us to believe his ancient lie—in the name of "harmony" and "peace" and anything else he might use to deceive us—and to join him in his rebellion against God.

Globalism vs. Nationalism

We touched on what a "one-world government" might look like in the previous chapter, but we should further examine the sudden dramatic push away from the traditional order of things, in which nations had sovereignty, and toward a new order of things in which "globalism" is the desired outcome. Of course, the boldest part of the lie at the heart of this is that "nationalism" leads to wars, and that some form of "globalism" will unite the world along wonderfully utopian lines. Precisely how that will happen must never be spelled out, nor can it be. But we do know that those who propose themselves as the leaders of this new globalist order do not believe in the sacred principles of the American Founding and are dedicated to crushing them forever. Their tack is not to speak of America in positive terms, but as an evil empire, causing harm whenever it has interfered with other nations. What these globalists have in mind for the world government they are planning certainly cannot coexist with America as we know her and cannot abide such quaint ideas as self-government and liberty and the sanctity of the individual. Nor can it coexist alongside the idea of our equality before the law and, more importantly, our equality in God's sight.

Many in the past have talked about "globalism." They usually used other terms, but the ideas have always been the same. Early in the twentieth century, there was the "League of Nations," and then after World War II, the "United Nations." But anyone who knows anything about that institution has observed the monstrous naïveté at the heart of it all and how it has been cynically used by nations who couldn't care less about human rights and would cherish nothing more than the idea of exterminating such concepts forever, just as Hitler and Stalin and other supremely evil leaders have tried to do. In the beginning, the UN spoke much about "freedom," as though that were the underlying goal. They even commissioned Norman Rockwell to create his famous illustrations of the "Four Freedoms." But all those comforting ideas have been quite forgotten in the decades since.

Nonetheless, the most dedicated globalists, who for decades seemed only to talk amongst themselves at impossibly posh gatherings, have made gigantic leaps forward of late and are doing all they can to enact the ghastly plans we have only recently heard about. Because of the COVID pandemic—whose origins many of those in the globalist circles have done all they can to obfuscate—many in America suddenly seemed eager to discard our national sovereignty as they joined anyone who purported to seek a "global solution." For the first time in American history, many in our own government did all they could along these lines, pushing hard for us to bow to the will of international organizations like the World Health Organization. Of course, no one in America ever voted for the faceless bureaucrats in that or similar organizations, but the sudden "health emergency" was used to override everything. We then discovered that the WHO and similar organizations were strongly allied with—if not entirely controlled by—China. The fact that China's Communist elites are profoundly and inherently opposed to American values—and would surely take over our nation if given the opportunity—seems to have been overlooked in the general madness.

In order for globalism to properly take root, one must first undermine the ideas of nationalism and national pride as positive things. Americans saw this for the first time during the presidency of Barack Obama, who when asked whether he believed in American "exceptionalism" essentially said that he did not. He gave a strange and tortured answer in which he said that he supposed he felt America was exceptional in the way that anyone thinks their own country is exceptional.[1] This was, of course, a cynical dodge. Every single person ought to be proud of his nation and of his culture to some extent; there can be no doubt of that. But for an American president to be unable to say that there was indeed something extraordinary and exceptional about America was unprecedented. There has never been a country in history that has been a beacon of liberty to the whole world and that has put itself forward as a "nation of nations," meant to live out what Jesus said and John Winthrop repeated and many presidents have cited ever since about being "a shining city on a hill." All of our Founders understood this view of America as an ideal that was ever in the process of refining itself and that held its hands out to the rest of the world whenever possible. Many around the world knew that was who we were at our Founding, and many have known it ever since. No American president saw this more clearly than Abraham Lincoln, who wrote and spoke of it often. And no American president until Barack Obama ever dissented from the idea. It is a curious and a worrisome development. What could be behind it?

The uniqueness of all nations and cultures—and especially that of the United States—has become anathema to any in the globalist camp, who have sometimes quite openly admitted that they prefer a one-world government in which they can be at the top of the pyramid. There is no question that their principal enemy is the United States—or at least those in America who still share the Founders' vision and values that we are all made by God to be free and derive our rights from Him, and that legitimate governments derive their rights from the governed. Therefore, those opposed to these American ideas (but who live in the United States) are very loudly and forcefully advocating for culturally Marxist ideas and have very happily allied themselves with globalists—and both groups have aligned themselves with Communist China.

For all these things to suddenly be possible has required many forces and trends over the decades. The rise of the "global economy"— always touted by those for whom "free markets" are not just a good thing but an idol—has given way to "multinational corporations" that do not believe in American values and have no fidelity to them, and that are now at the forefront in pushing these other developments. When a Google or an Apple or a Nike or a Facebook or an Amazon realizes that it can become more powerful by working with Communist China—and perhaps even by developing technologies that Chinese leaders will use to subjugate their own populations as virtual slaves—who is to stop them? We know that many industrialists made fortunes working with pro-slavery Confederates in the nineteenth century, and that many more in the twentieth century made fortunes doing business with Nazi Germany. This is when the "free market" is divorced from morality and, rather than being a force for good, becomes a force for evil. If you take God and virtue out of the equation with regard to market forces, the result is the same as when you take God and virtue out of the equation with regard to democratic elections. The American Founders knew that genuine freedom was only possible with a "virtuous citizenry"—so what happens when freedom is unmoored from virtue and those values to which we have always subscribed? The answer is what we are now seeing, and it is nothing less than the triumph of evil.

We have seen what happens when tremendously powerful pharmaceutical corporations ally themselves with these forces, as they did during the aforementioned pandemic, to make it extremely difficult for anyone to find alternatives to their products. Social media giants and corporate media giants have also helped push these evils forward, as does everyone on the political left—and many on the political right, too.

There is no question that the technology we now possess is what has made all these things possible. The ability to use our phones and other devices to keep track of our movements and of how and where we spend our money is unlike anything we have ever encountered, and adds to the sense that forces beyond our control are to some extent controlling us and working very hard to do so much more definitively. Our ability now to move billions of dollars electronically in the "cashless society" Alex Jones and others mentioned decades ago has become a reality and has made it possible for nameless banks and other financial entities to shut down people's ability to control their own money, as we have seen many times in the past three years alone. Freedom-loving dissenters who try to exercise their freedoms may find that it is impossible for them to do business.

This is an utterly astonishing moment in world history. What are we to do about it? Can we help but think of the verses in Revelation about those who refused to bow down to "the Beast" being unable to buy or sell?

We are in a new era in this global economy, and there can be no doubt that the checks and balances against the abuse of power are not there. There can be no doubt that the accrual of power by a handful of bad actors is now possible in a way it has never been possible in the history of the world. And it is not only possible, but already happening, dramatically and quickly. All these things taken together represent a nightmarish and absolutely unprecedented moment in the history of our species.

If these powerful trends continue, can there be any doubt that we will lose every one of the cherished, God-given rights that our Founders created a government to protect? We already are beginning to lose them, and more quickly than any of us could have imagined— just as the Germans under Hitler were astonished at how quickly the world they took for granted vanished. The German church was their only hope then, and the American church is our only hope now. There is no other cultural institution powerful enough to mount any defense. Is your church part of that, or are you attending a church that wishes it would all simply go away and seems to be convinced that it's not their job to be part of battling such things?

Either way, the fact remains that we in America cannot remain a self-governing people if globalist elites continue using everything in their power to impose their will upon us in this authoritarian way—brazenly flouting all our traditions and the ideas of a "government of the people, by the people, for the people"—and unless the American church burns its boats and lives out a "religionless Christianity" that has no fear of death, knowing that Jesus really did defeat death on the Cross—just as Bonhoeffer knew, and lived accordingly.

Apart from God's intervention via His remnant Church, we seem headed rather inevitably toward the nightmare of the one-world government described in Revelation, run by a cabal of elites who have sometimes discreetly and sometimes openly allied themselves with demons. Alas, that is not an overstatement of the case. It is where we are presently headed unless you—who are the Church—do all that is within your power against these things.

CHAPTER THIRTEEN

Bonhoeffer's Moment of Failure

*And we know that for those who love God all things
work together for good, for those who are called
according to his purpose.*

—*Romans 8:28*

Many people who have read my biography of Bonhoeffer have been so moved by the true story of his heroism that they put him on a pedestal, as though he were perfect, which we should know he was not. It's human nature to unwittingly transform heroic historical figures into fictional figures whose exploits are so beyond what we ourselves might ever achieve that they essentially give us permission not to try. We pretend that it is somehow noble and virtuous of us to say that we could never be in the league of the hero about whom we are reading. But as important as it is to be humble, it is equally important to share God's opinion of us. God says that we can do *all things* through Him who strengthens us. If you don't believe that, you are not exercising humility but rather a "religious" objection to what God Himself has declared and fall into the trap of being fatalistic. When that happens, we end up using our religious excuse to participate in Satan's plan for us rather than God's.

127

This is fiction—and even worse, it is actually a harmful lie. We may do this with figures from the Scriptures, such as David or Moses or Paul, thinking them so far beyond what we are capable of that we don't take seriously God's call for us to be like them in our own time and in our own spheres. For this reason, the Scriptures make a point of telling us that both David and Moses were murderers, and that Paul stood by while giving his approval to the murder of Stephen. We are *all* sinners; pretending that our heroes are superheroes is a tactic of the enemy to prevent us from doing God's will in our own lives. God graciously shows us that the very greatest spiritual heroes—apart from Jesus—had moments of crushing failure, and Bonhoeffer was no different.

In early 1933, just months after the Nazis had taken power, Bonhoeffer was asked to preach the funeral sermon of his twin sister Sabine's father-in-law, who was a Jew. Sabine's husband Gerhard had converted to Christianity, as so many Jews in Germany had done over the decades and centuries, but his father had not. The timing was very bad, and Bonhoeffer was in a difficult spot. No one knew what the future held, and Bonhoeffer didn't want to be incendiary if he could avoid it. He wanted to be able to continue to speak against the Nazi policies and continue to fight against what was happening, since there was still time to succeed. To preach at the funeral of a Jewish man at a supremely ticklish moment such as that was all his enemies needed to demonize him and silence him forever. (In today's parlance, we would call it "canceling" him.)

As he mulled over this request, he was urged to consult with his theological superiors, so he spoke to his "district superintendent" about it. Perhaps predictably, his superintendent didn't want to court the trouble this action might cause and very strongly advised Bonhoeffer to forego preaching this funeral sermon. Bonhoeffer understood the logic and complied with the request not to preach. The idea was, of course, that he had bigger fish to fry. There was no reason to court trouble and scotch his ability to attend to more important things. It was simple prudence, so he graciously declined Sabine and Gerhard's request.

But as Bonhoeffer saw things deteriorating rapidly around him in the months that followed, he felt that he had made a terrible mistake. Perhaps if he had preached at that funeral, it would have sent precisely the right strong message to the Nazis—and to the anti-Semites within the church—that would have helped the situation. In any case, Bonhoeffer felt that his decision not to preach at that funeral had been a mistake, and a shameful one at that. So in late October 1933, he wrote a letter to his sister and her husband, apologizing:

> I am tormented even now by the thought that I didn't do as you asked me, as a matter of course. To be frank, I can't think what made me behave as I did. How could I have been so horribly afraid at the time? It must have seemed equally incomprehensible to you both, and yet you said nothing. But it preys on my mind, because it's the kind of thing one can never make up for. So all I can do is ask you to forgive my weakness then. I know now for certain that I ought to have behaved differently.[1]

Bonhoeffer saw that being bold and defiant by preaching that funeral sermon would have sent an important signal not just to the Nazis that those in the church would stand with the Jews and not go along with the Nazis bullying, but also to the Jews that Christians would stand up for and with them. And it would have given confidence to those Christians who were dithering and needed to see someone boldly and fearlessly living out what he believed. But at the time, Bonhoeffer had not seen this; he even describes himself as having been "so horribly afraid" at that time. We don't think of Bonhoeffer of being capable of fear, and yet he confesses to his sister and her husband that it had indeed been at work in his heart.

Romans 8:28 says that "all things work together for good, for those who are called according to his purpose." So we can see that God—in allowing Bonhoeffer to make this mistake early on—could use it to galvanize him against similar actions in the future. We can only imagine how many times afterward Bonhoeffer was bolder than he might have otherwise been if he didn't have this mistake to haunt him as an example of how not to behave.

And his mistake is good news for the rest of us now, because it is crucial to see that even the great Dietrich Bonhoeffer was a human being just as we are, and he was someone who, like any one of us, could be tempted to do the wrong thing. So the question is not whether any of us can be tempted to do the wrong thing. The question is whether we—like Bonhoeffer—can be made to see that we have done the wrong thing and repent of it. That is the Christian path forward. Ours is a God of redemption and forgiveness, and He alone can show us the way forward when we have stumbled.

How many pastors do we know in our own time who have done things like that? Just as Bonhoeffer was persuaded, they too were genuinely persuaded that what they were doing—or not doing—was the prudent course. Perhaps, for example, when the mayor of their town or the governor of their state overstepped his or her authority and required churches to shut down, they thought it was right to comply—sometimes doing so in the name of "showing honor" to those civic or state leaders. Perhaps they didn't consider that the spiritual health of their parishioners was also at stake and must be prioritized. Or perhaps they found some way around the governmental bullying that enabled them not to directly confront that mayor or governor and somehow to step aside in this battle they were not prepared or willing to fight. Or perhaps they even stood so firmly with the mayor or governmental authorities that they condemned other churches that were not inclined to comply, treating their dissenting brethren as troublemakers who were not representing God's purposes in the situation. Can they now see that they did not act ideally in the situation, and might they be willing to repent? And will we forgive them if they do, as Christ has forgiven us?

Before my most recent book, *Letter to the American Church*, was scheduled to come out, I was invited to speak to a congregation about it. That evening was the first time I laid eyes on physical copies of the book. Because I wasn't sure where the leadership of this church stood on the issues I was discussing—and because I hadn't yet spoken about the issues detailed in the book to a live audience—I was a little bit diffident about how I framed things. But I know that what I said must have resonated with the pastor, because as I was preparing to leave afterward, he caught me in the parking lot and asked if we could chat. He essentially confessed that what I had said had gotten to him—had convicted him—and he then told me a story which reminds me of Bonhoeffer's story about the funeral.

This pastor said he had recently felt a duty to speak out at a city council meeting in his district against some genuinely awful legislation being forced on local schools regarding what they would teach kids about sexuality. He knew that most parents would be outraged about it, and as a local pastor, he felt obliged to show up at the meeting and speak against it. But the eldership at his church had different ideas and strongly told him he must not do that. Their stance was so unequivocal that he thought it best to accede to what they were saying—so he did not go to the meeting and did not speak up. And as it happened, the awful legislation passed. One cannot know whether his presence and voice would have changed that, but when he told me this story, it was obvious that he felt horrible about letting the wishes of his elders keep him from doing what he thought to be right.

I was privileged not only to hear this man's confession of what he saw as his own failure, but to tell him that if he now saw what he had done as a lost opportunity, he could at least make sure that he would not lose another in the future. Like Bonhoeffer, his failure to do the right thing at one point didn't mean he wouldn't be given other opportunities. Indeed, perhaps his sense of failure in that one instance would encourage him to look for other opportunities in which he could do the right thing and be a voice for truth in a time when such voices are rare. Perhaps when that opportunity came, his speaking out would encourage others to speak out, and their voices would encourage still others.

Only the enemy wants us to despair and give up. God always wants to encourage us to acknowledge our mistakes and to move on from them, resolved to do the right thing when we next have an opportunity to do so.

CHAPTER FOURTEEN

Be Greatly Encouraged

That we are heading toward a one-world government and a one-world religion is hardly encouraging news—unless we look to God. And unless we obey God. We need to know what we are facing, but we also need to know that succumbing to these forces is not inevitable if we turn utterly to Jesus and self-sacrificially do what He asks of us. God most clearly calls us to a "religionless Christianity" when nothing else will suffice, and He is in this hour calling us—those who have ears to hear—to precisely that. He is raising up His holy remnant and calling us to join Him in the battle between good and evil, for which we were both born and born-again. God has allowed we who are His Church to play a central role in how all these things play out.

What we face is impossible without God—but isn't anything worth doing impossible without God? We may not know whether we will succeed, but surely we know that even if we are destined to fail, we must fail while fighting, out of joyful obedience to the One Who calls us to the battle. Jesus said, "Apart from me you can do nothing," but the Scriptures also proclaim that we can "do all things through" Him "who strengthens us." God wants to encourage us to join Him with great joy and boldness.

It seems that more and more people are waking up to where we are and are willing to step out in their faith in a new way. But we must ask: Why do so many still continue to hang back? Why do so many still attend churches that are blind to the rising evils around us, as so many in Germany did in the 1930s? Why are so many Christians still neutered into inaction and silence and submission to the evil Spirit of the Age? What are we afraid of?

Have You Drunk the Kool-Aid of Secularism?

Though we have touched on this throughout the book, let's return to Bonhoeffer's 1928 diagnosis of "secularization." This phenomenon has only increased in the American church since he spoke of it: We voluntarily restrict our faith to a religious corner but otherwise go along with the secular views of the unbelieving world. In that 1928 lecture, Bonhoeffer said the church had pushed Christ out of its faith, leaving them with an empty husk of religiosity. But this is even more true today. We may go to church, but apart from that and a few religious activities, we have become essentially secular. We may not believe the whole secularist narrative, but we often act as though we do, and have unwittingly allowed it to dilute our faith. Consequently, we are not so bold about our faith. Our confidence somehow has been shaken.

So what is the fundamental secular narrative?

It is simply that there is no God. But what follows from this falsehood touches and affects absolutely everything, just as our belief in God is meant to touch and affect everything. To the extent that we do not carry our faith into every sphere, we are tacitly accepting not just one satanic lie, but a host of them. Of course, the secular view presents itself as somehow neutral, as though the idea that there is no God is only one small point. But the idea that there is no God really does affect everything and must therefore be boldly rejected with every atom of our being. But are Christians doing that and expressing their faith in every sphere? The question is whether we really unequivocally know that God is God and the Bible is true. Do we? Or are we rather hedging our bets by keeping silent and essentially going along with the lies that follow from the secular version of things?

For example, the idea that there is no God pushes forward the lie that science is at odds with biblical faith. This lie relies on a number of wildly preposterous ideas that many in the church quietly accept. For example, it says that every human being in history "emerged" from non-life and nothingness by accident. It says that inanimate, blind forces somehow, in their everlasting sloshing, came to "create" what we now call life, despite the fact that the simplest cell in the universe is heart-stoppingly complex. It also says that life somehow "evolved" upward into all the life on the planet now, including yours and mine. So because our existence is perfectly accidental, it therefore logically and unavoidably follows that it has zero intrinsic value or meaning. According to this secular view, a mother or a father or a child has precisely the same value as a cow or an anchovy or an amoeba—or a lifeless rock—which is to say, it has absolutely none. This is an astonishingly radical belief, and manifestly absurd. But it lies at the heart of all secularism. There is no logical way around it, though most secularists cannot bear to admit it any more than Adolf Hitler would in 1932 have explicitly announced the fundamentals of his own philosophy, lest someone be able to see the hellscape to which such fundamentals inevitably must lead.

But this secular narrative has been pushed so hard for so long that many ostensible Christians have, to some extent, given it a place in their lives. They—we—have drunk enough of the secular Kool-Aid that we often aren't so sure what we believe. At least, we aren't sure enough to be wild and bold and loud and active about it, especially on "controversial" subjects. We are therefore more inclined to be quiet, to be "faithful witnesses" as some have put it, but who often actually behave like frightened rabbits, hoping the ravening dogs don't notice us—or hoping they notice us last. Even though we identify as Christians, we have believed many lies about the faith, and it is this complicity of God's people with the secular narrative that must change dramatically and quickly. If it doesn't, we won't be able to do what God requires of us in this most crucial of historical hours.

This is precisely why we need to name and reject these secular lies—which are atheistic and ultimately demonic—and remind ourselves of the truth over and over. We need to remember the truths that we have forgotten, or mostly forgotten, and must proclaim them and all that follows from them. We need to understand that they really are true, so that we don't merely "believe" they are true or "hope" they are true, but actually *know* they are true.

So what are those truths?

Jesus Changes Everything

For starters, the Bible is really true. It really is the Word of God, and not a collection of fables and moral injunctions. God really is the Author of all that exists, and really is omniscient and omnipresent and omnipotent. He is alive and speaks to us today.

Beyond this, we must know that when Christians have truly lived out their faith along the lines of what we are calling "religionless

Christianity," endless good has resulted throughout history. Jesus changes everything. The secular narrative has portrayed the Christian faith as many negative things, from being a colonialist, power-hungry, negative force in history to a moralistic ideology that wants to keep people from experiencing joy. Of course, bastardized versions of Christian faith have been guilty of some of these things, which we sometimes have confused with the real version of the Christian faith. But what we are calling "religionless Christianity" has always been a dramatic and revolutionary force for good. This is undeniable historical fact, but do we in the church know it well enough not to be cowed into silence on it?

Wherever Christians have brought their faith out of the caves and church buildings on Sunday morning and into the light of day in the public sphere every day of the week, we see dramatic improvement in people's lives. The facts of history on this score are astonishing and desperately need to be known. They have been recounted in many books by many people, including friends of mine such as Dinesh D'Souza and Vishal Mangalwadi, to name but two. The secular narrative needs to be boldly denounced not merely as false, but as a pernicious lie that has harmed billions of human beings throughout history.

For example, we must remind ourselves and declare that only the biblical view of the human person gives us the radical idea that we should care for the poor and the sick. Only the Old and New Testaments tell us that we are all absolutely equal in God's sight. Therefore, racism is wrong, as is treating women as second-class citizens. Atheists and secularists have no idea why these things are wrong, or even that they really are wrong. They have no basis upon which to say that anything is right or wrong. This is a supremely well-hidden and unbelievably embarrassing fact. Only the Bible can be the foundation for human dignity, as every single human being is made in God's image. And only the Bible helps us to see the obligation of those of us who have power, wealth, and freedom to use those things to help those less fortunate than ourselves. These are radical ideas in human history, and they come only from the Bible—though they have been stolen by secularists who hope no one will notice. But we need to notice and speak of it loudly and boldly, and never cease speaking of it.

Did you know that in Europe in the fourth century, when Emperor Constantine ended the persecution of Christians—so that for the first time in human history, Christianity was allowed to flourish—hospitals to care for the sick bloomed all across Europe, run by nuns and monks? Did you know that apart from cultures animated by biblical ideas, the weak and sick are generally thought "cursed" and left to die—which is in perfect accordance with what Darwinists came to call "survival of the fittest"? Did you know that it was the Christian faith that gave rise to the ideas of the university and academic freedom? Did you know that the first university was begun by monks in the eleventh century? Or that the Christian faith gave us the idea of objective truth, or that it is God's will that we use science to investigate the world He created, to His glory?

In my book *Is Atheism Dead?* I explain how science increasingly points to God and how the more we discover through it, the more we see there is simply no possibility whatsoever that everything emerged by accident. In our own lifetimes, the scientific evidence for God has become impossible to deny. But did you know that? Or have you bought the secular narrative that science is somehow pushing God further and further away from us, into the realm of myth and legend? Did you know that it was devout Christians in the sixteenth and seventeenth centuries who created what we call the scientific method and modern science? Not only is science compatible with faith—and faith with science—but science itself came about precisely because of Christianity, which is the very antithesis of the lie that secularists have been trumpeting for two centuries.

Did you know that it was only because of Christians boldly bringing biblical values into the public sphere that inhuman cruelty and slavery is now universally condemned in the West, and only exists today in radical Muslim countries and atheist states like China and North Korea? In the eighteenth century, it was because of William Wilberforce and other outspoken evangelical Christians behaving politically that the transatlantic slave trade was abolished. It was because of Wilberforce acting politically that India was made to end the sickening practice of "suttee," in which widows were burned alive on the funeral pyres of their dead husbands. Indeed, as a result of Wilberforce's leadership, Christians in the early nineteenth century became so politically and culturally active on a host of fronts that the whole idea that we ought to have a social conscience and care for those less fortunate than ourselves became the standard view in the West. Most atheists and agnostics have accepted this despite having no idea why; nor do they grasp that their own view actually militates against this humane standard.

Did you know that it was because of Bible-thumping believers in America that the abolition movement came into being, transforming a nation that countenanced the evil of chattel slavery into a nation that outlawed it forever? And did you know it was because of the civil rights movement—which was birthed in American churches—that the biblical view on race was brought to bear throughout our nation via federal legislation outlawing Jim Crow laws?

All of these things represent the smallest handful of highlights of the larger narrative, but it is long past time that we who call ourselves

Christians not only know these things, but live as though we know them and challenge the secularists boldly. If we know that our faith really does bless people, how dare we be shy about sharing it and carrying it into every sphere possible?

Dare We Dream?

As I mention in *Is Atheism Dead?*, I write about much of the relatively recent—and generally unknown or suppressed—evidence for the God of the Bible. There is no question that it is astonishing and that most Christians are unaware of it. Along the lines of this chapter, reading it will embolden you in your faith. This ever-growing tide of evidence has come to be so incontrovertible that it really cannot be overstated, and I myself was quite unaware of much of it. In the face of this evidence, we are not only profoundly bolstered in our own faith, but will come to see we cannot help but regard anyone calling himself an atheist the same way we regard someone claiming to believe the earth is flat. The stubborn facts cannot any longer support either theory, and to countenance either one seriously is to participate in a kind of madness. No one wants to be insulting or insensitive to those with whom we disagree, but at what point in going along with now quite patent untruths are we guilty of bearing false witness? At what point, if we pretend to take such ideas seriously, are we guilty of not loving the person with whom we are speaking?

In writing that book, I began to wonder whether I myself had been guilty not merely of having drunk some of the secular Kool-Aid, but to some extent of ceasing to believe that God might again move in history in a positive way, as though He could never undo and reverse the false secularist narrative. In writing the book, I saw that the evidence for God emerging in this very hour is so overwhelming, that we should seriously ask whether it might portend revival—and not merely revival, but perhaps another Great Awakening. Even more than that, it might well augur a new Renaissance and Reformation, so that we should work and pray toward that end. I realized I had been guilty of accepting the idea that we must forever live in a world where everyone believes science is at odds with Christian faith, where everyone believes the Bible to be an outdated and uninspired collection of exaggerated or flatly untrue stories. I had forgotten that with God, all things are possible, and that these seemingly immovable secular falsehoods might conceivably be debunked, just as other things we held to be immovable givens throughout history have been debunked and radically overturned.

We must ask ourselves whether we dare to hope that our bold resistance to evil might not merely allow us to avoid the horrors the German church faced in the 1930s, but might actually lead us to a world in which the idea that there is no God is widely and firmly rejected, just as slavery is widely and firmly rejected today. We must dare to hope that the false secular narratives will not merely fail to triumph and lead us to an End Time dystopia, but might be so thoroughly debunked that they would lead to a new era that is mostly unimaginable to us today.

Many of us have simply accepted the dark status quo and forgotten what God might yet do. We earlier called that worshiping a religious idol of fatalism. Can we not hope and pray that God isn't finished with us, and that He has good things yet to do in history?

Wasn't just such a lack of hope what tempted many of us to accept the Soviet Union as an immovable given enduring into the distant future? Weren't many tempted to "make peace" with the evil of that soulless empire and to not envision a world in which freedom triumphed? In the final chapter of *Letter to the American Church*, I discuss how it took boldness, vision, and faith—and a godly willingness to fight against evil—for the Iron Curtain to be rent asunder, which by God's grace it finally was. But how many could not be enticed to hope toward that end and therefore did nothing? How many could not imagine what finally actually happened in 1989 and 1991, when the Berlin Wall fell and the Soviet Union broke apart and ceased to exist? Similarly, how many of us were guilty of being unable to imagine that the unjust and unconstitutional ruling in *Roe v. Wade* could ever actually be overturned, and therefore did not even vote so that it might be? Why did we accept the satanic lies that desperately fought to keep the Iron Curtain and *Roe v. Wade* in place forever? Why did we let a fatalistic view of things stymie us into silence and inaction?

But these are only our more recent failures of imagination—which are actually failures to live out our faith in every sphere. Throughout history, there have been many. How many believers two and a half centuries ago shrank from believing that a nation that stood for liberty and justice for all really could emerge, and therefore did not join the battle to make it a reality? How many believers shrank from thinking slavery could ever be abolished, and saw it as a necessary evil that had always existed and always would? How many could not imagine that Israel might again become a nation after two thousand years?

The question comes to us again now. Have we lost hope that God really might still do great things as He has done in the past? Have we accepted what we see as impossible to change? Dare we hope and pray and fight toward what God might wish to do? Or do we look at the circumstances around us and fatalistically declare that trying to fight is not worth our trouble and that—among other things—America is finished?

To better see where we are now, we must return to when America began.

CONCLUSION

It was the summer of 1776. Things were looking inescapably bleak for George Washington and the Continental Army under his command. We know his odds of success against the greatest army in the world were decidedly long, to the extent that apart from a genuine miracle or series of such, the emergence into history of a nation based on the ideas of liberty and self-government was already doomed. If someone had asked him his assessment of things at that juncture, how might he have answered?

Washington understood that the prospects before him were grim. But from everything we know of him, it is clear that he would have answered that "if Providence be for us" in the cause of liberty, the colonists may yet prevail. Therefore, they fought on. Washington knew that if the God of history—who acted in history—was for them, success was possible; apart from that, there was little reason to hope. But he also knew that the only path forward required fighting. Whether they ultimately succeeded or failed, many young men would die that summer, and their families would never see them again. They could not know the future, but they would continue to pray and fight and hope.

Washington did not then foresee the terrible winter at Valley Forge, with men freezing and tracking blood as they walked barefoot upon the Pennsylvania snow. He did not foresee how long and difficult things would be, and he did not foresee the eventual victory that Providence deigned to bequeath him several years later. But of course, today we know that at Yorktown in October 1781, it happened.

But it is principally because the American cause of independence *did* succeed that we have forgotten that the colonists really might have failed ignominiously. We forget that by all natural expectations, this nation ought never to have been born, and instead, ought to have been murdered in the womb. So we forget to marvel that it was born, and that it grew, and that it endured, even unto this hour. Because we must never forget these things, we must take pains to remind ourselves of them and teach them to our children.

We must not simply remember the tremendous improbability of the triumph of liberty at that time. We must also remember how few chose to risk their lives in fighting with Washington. We must remember that the majority of those living in the colonies at that time were either simply bystanders in the conflict—somehow sitting on the fence to see which way things went—or were Tories who sided with our enemy, Great Britain. We must remember this because little has changed since then. Only a fraction of our population gave their all, despite the fact that millions—including us today—would benefit from what they gave. We have forgotten, too, that as a result of their sacrifice, a nation came into existence that would do immeasurable good, not least by showing the world that people could live freely and govern themselves. Nor should we forget that as a result of the faith and prosperity that we have had, we send more missionaries around the world than any other nation, and innumerable souls have come into God's Kingdom as a result. We are obliged to remember that God Himself brought our nation into the world—and that it was not for our purposes, but for His.

We should also remember Lincoln's words at Gettysburg, that we are a nation "conceived in liberty and dedicated to the proposition that all men are created equal," not least because these are unavoidably biblical ideas that do not follow from a secular view of things. In that famous speech, Lincoln said the war in which we were engaged at that time was a "test" to determine whether a nation so dedicated could "endure," and that he was himself as unsure whether it could endure as Washington was whether it would come into existence in the first place. Both men publicly averred that it was a matter of God's will, and both knew that tremendous sacrifices must be made in the process.

So we return at last to the idea we put forward in this book's introduction: that we are today in a great existential crisis, which is the third—and likely final one—of our history. What we face in America today presents as impossible a prospect as Washington or Lincoln faced, with ramifications every bit as dramatic for the whole world. We face forces from within and without that are devoutly dedicated to eradicating all Washington and Lincoln and every patriot in our history held dear and fought for. Can we deny that those two previous crises had great historical consequences far beyond our shores? Can we deny that the future of the whole world was at stake in those conflicts, although those who fought in them could hardly have foreseen it?

So, too, we must see that the nature of the crisis in which we find ourselves at this time goes far beyond our own nation. Those who understand our history and the God of history know that He did not create and then preserve America merely for Americans. Our birth into history and our continued existence has ultimately been for the benefit of those beyond our shores. Although we are not "officially" Christian, our vision of ourselves has always been distinctly and unavoidably Christian, especially along these lines.

As John Winthrop—quoting Jesus—preached in 1630, we in America were to be as "a city set upon a hill" for all the world to see. We were to shine so brightly that those beholding us from afar would see that we were different and would either want to come here to partake of our liberties or replicate it in their own lands. If we conducted ourselves worthily, our example would lead people to the God we worshiped. So if God blesses anyone—whether a person or a nation—He blesses them to be a blessing to others. Therefore, what is at stake now concerns not merely us, but the whole world.

Winthrop's sermon before his congregation boarded their ship to head across the Atlantic for Boston is worth quoting:

> For we must consider that we shall be as a city upon a hill. The eyes of all people are upon us. So that if we shall deal falsely with our God in this work we have undertaken, and so cause Him to withdraw His present help from us, we shall be made a story and a by-word through the world. We shall open the mouths of enemies to speak evil of the ways of God, and all professors for God's sake. We shall shame the faces of many of God's worthy servants, and cause their prayers to be turned into curses upon us till we be consumed out of the good land whither we are going.

And to shut this discourse with that exhortation of Moses, that faithful servant of the Lord, in his last farewell to Israel, Deut. 30. "Beloved, there is now set before us life and death, good and evil," in that we are commanded this day to love the Lord our God, and to love one another, to walk in his ways and to keep his Commandments and his ordinance and his laws, and the articles of our Covenant with Him, that we may live and be multiplied, and that the Lord our God may bless us in the land whither we go to possess it. But if our hearts shall turn away, so that we will not obey, but shall be seduced, and worship other Gods, our pleasure and profits, and serve them; it is propounded unto us this day, we shall surely perish out of the good land whither we pass over this vast sea to possess it.

Therefore let us choose life, that we and our seed may live, by obeying His voice and cleaving to Him, for He is our life and our prosperity.[1]

This view of things has always been God's calling on America—and at the heart of this high calling, indisputably, is the American church. Our Founders understood this, and after them, Tocqueville and Lincoln and many others understood it. So the question before us now is whether we who call ourselves by God's name will rise to this crisis with everything we have, living out our faith as though we actually believe it with our whole hearts.

God gave us victory in our first and second existential crises, but what we face in this one is in some ways more explicitly about Him than the first two were. God's avowed enemies are far more present in this conflict and more explicit in their hatred of Him and His people. So now, more than ever, it falls to God's people to lead the way. But can we imagine what God might do if we are faithful to Him as we never have been before?

Even those who are not believers but are simply patriotic Americans who understand the sacrifices made for us and our children in our history seem to sense that what we are facing now is existential—a battle between good and evil in the world. How can those of us who call ourselves Christians not see that it is our duty to do all we can while we can? It would be "religious" of us—in the negative sense of that word as we have been using it—not to see that the sacrifices of every patriot, including those unaware of God's hand, deserve a response from us at this moment in history. Lincoln concluded his Gettysburg address with these words:

> It is rather for us to be here dedicated to the great task remaining before us—that from these honored dead we take increased devotion to that cause for which they gave the last full measure of devotion—that we here highly resolve that these dead shall not have died in vain—that this nation, under God, shall have a new birth of freedom—and that government of the people, by the people, for the people, shall not perish from the earth.[2]

Can we doubt that God was speaking through the humble rail-splitter on that battlefield? So much has been written about what Lincoln said that day. But we would add one more thing: In his use of the words "a new birth of freedom," might Lincoln have been speaking prophetically? What if those words were meant for us today, to call us forward into this battle so that we could, in our nation, in our time, see "a new birth of freedom"?

Anyone familiar with the tumultuous period following Lincoln's murder, from the broken promises of Reconstruction through the Jim Crow era and into our own time, knows that we have not yet seen the "new birth of freedom" Lincoln spoke of that day. But can we imagine that all we are struggling for now might result not merely in "keeping the Republic" (to quote Benjamin Franklin) or in the further "endurance" of the nation (in Lincoln's words), but in something far greater, so that the whole world would marvel? Can we imagine that those words were prophetic for us now?

Similarly, can we imagine that Bonhoeffer's wistful use of the phrase "religionless Christianity"—which he himself would not see lived out—was a prophetic word for us now, to call us higher and deeper for God's history-changing purposes in this generation? Can we ask whether Bonhoeffer's words in that letter were somehow for us today, just as we have asked whether Lincoln's words were intended by God for us now?

When Bonhoeffer wrote of "religionless Christianity," he knew that the church in Germany had failed. But the question implied in his remarking on this—and in using that phrase—is whether there might be a time when God's church would not fail and when it would, as a result of heeding His call, stand heroically against evil. Would this not bring about an extraordinary transformation in history, like a second Reformation? What would that transformation look like?

We might for our purposes imagine that the Church has existed in history principally as a caterpillar whose ultimate telos, everyone knows, is to become a butterfly, but which it has not yet become. Bonhoeffer hoped to call the Church in his time to cease from its mere religion, to cease from merely playing church and to truly be the

Church, and thus to stand against the evil of that day. But of course, we know that when the crisis came and God spoke, the church of that day chose to remain what we might call a religious caterpillar. It was unwilling to become at that time what it was born to become, and evil triumphed.

But might it not have been God speaking this phrase through Bonhoeffer eighty years ago as a prophetic promise to us now? Can we imagine that as a result of the horrors of our present darkness, we would at last hear God's call to live our faith as Bonhoeffer wished his fellow believers had done in his day? Can we imagine that God is calling us to make the transformation into what we are meant to be in history before He returns to end history forever?

We know God called Moses to lead His people out of Egypt and through the Red Sea, and we know that two thousand years ago, He sent His Messiah into this world to lead it to worship the God of Israel. Can we not imagine that He is again doing a new thing in history? Can anyone who knows that God did something extraordinary at Pentecost—or who believes He did something extraordinary five hundred years ago in Wittenberg, or a century ago at Azusa Street—not believe He may yet do dramatic things in history for His purposes?

Can we imagine that if we dare to answer His call to be transformed as He would transform us, that we might via our newfound wings arise to confront the evil of our time in a way otherwise impossible and unimaginable?

Why should we not allow ourselves to believe that God caused Bonhoeffer to write those two words so that eighty years in the future, He might speak to us through them? Would God not wish to use the example of the German church's failure to goad us now to repent of our own failure so that we might be those who answered His call and enabled Him to do what He has longed to do in human history?

We must wonder what would happen if God's people right now really and truly believed what is true and really and truly behaved with the abandon and freedom that comes from that real faith. What would happen if we stopped piously hoping that God has defeated Death, but actually knew that He has done so—and lived that way? That was Bonhoeffer's wistful dream in writing the two words that are the title of this book. He knew that if we would embrace a "religionless Christianity," we really would defeat the evil that is otherwise impossible to defeat and see God's glory in our generation. Do we understand that is God's will for us now, and are we willing to do what is necessary to bring it about? Do we understand that a great revival—and much more—are His will for us? That is the question. We who are His Church must joyfully answer God's call to us now. When we do, we will see His hand in ways we have not imagined.

May God grant us the fulfillment of His dream in our time, to His glory. Amen.

Notes

Chapter Two: Bonhoeffer's Diagnosis

1. Eric Metaxas, *Bonhoeffer: Pastor, Martyr, Prophet, Spy* (Nashville: Thomas Nelson, 2010), 82.
2. Ibid.
3. Ibid.
4. Ibid.
5. Ibid., 82–83.
6. Ibid., 83.
7. Dietrich Bonhoeffer, *The Cost of Discipleship* (New York: Touchstone, 1959), 46–47.
8. Ibid., 49.
9. Ibid., 35–47.

Chapter Five: The Cautionary Tale of Martin Niemöller

1. Metaxas, *Bonhoeffer: Pastor, Martyr, Prophet, Spy*, 211.
2. Eric Metaxas, *Bonhoeffer Abridged: Pastor, Martyr, Prophet, Spy* (Nashville: Thomas Nelson, 2014), 87.

Chapter Seven: Further Thoughts on Cancel Culture

1. CNN, "Kirk Cameron Says, 'Homosexuality Is Unnatural,'" YouTube, March 2, 2012, https://www.youtube.com/watch?v=JhGQUKoH_TE.
2. Jessica Derschowitz, "Kirk Cameron Faces Backlash over Anti-Gay Remarks," CBS News, March 6, 2012, https://www.cbsnews.com/news/kirk-cameron-faces-backlash-over-anti-gay-remarks.

Chapter Nine: Bonhoeffer Burns His Boats

1. Metaxas, *Bonhoeffer: Pastor, Martyr, Prophet, Spy,* 337.
2. Rodney Combs, *Bonhoeffer's Cost of Discipleship, Shepherd's Notes* (Broadman and Holman Reference, 1999), 32.
3. Bonhoeffer, *The Cost of Discipleship*, 99.
4. "Sermon on Wisdom 3:3" in Dietrich Bonhoeffer, *Dietrich Bonhoeffer Works*, vol. 13, *London, 1933–1935* (Minneapolis: Fortress Press, 2007), 335.

Chapter Ten: Mere "Religion" vs. Following God

1. Metaxas, *Bonhoeffer: Pastor, Martyr, Prophet, Spy,* 359.
2. Ibid., 376.

Chapter Twelve: Resurrecting the Tower of Babel

1. James Kirchick, "Squanderer in Chief," *Los Angeles Times*, April 28, 2009, https://www.latimes.com/archives/la-xpm-2009-apr-28-oe-kirchick28-story.html.

Chapter Thirteen: Bonhoeffer's Moment of Failure

1. Metaxas, *Bonhoeffer: Pastor, Martyr, Prophet, Spy,* 160.

Conclusion

1. John Winthrop, "A Model of Christian Charity," in *A Library of American Literature: Early Colonial Literature, 1607-1675*, eds. Edmund Clarence Stedman and Ellen Mackay Hutchinson (New York: 1892), 304–307.
2. Abraham Lincoln, "The Gettysburg Address," November 19, 1863, https://usa.usembassy.de/etexts/speeches/getty.htm.

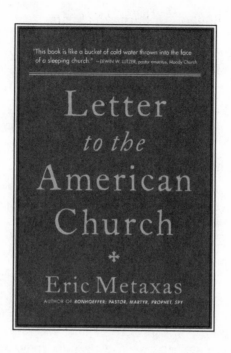

"This book is like a bucket of cold water thrown into the face of a sleeping church." —ERWIN W. LUTZER, pastor emeritus, Moody Church

Letter
to the
American
Church

✢

Eric Metaxas

AUTHOR OF *BONHOEFFER: PASTOR, MARTYR, PROPHET, SPY*

An earnest and searing wake-up call, Eric Metaxas's best-selling *Letter to the American Church* warns of the haunting similarities between today's American church and the German church of the 1930s. Echoing Bonhoeffer's prophetic call, Metaxas exhorts his fellow Christians to repent of their silence in the face of evil before it is too late.

DOCUMENTARY FILM

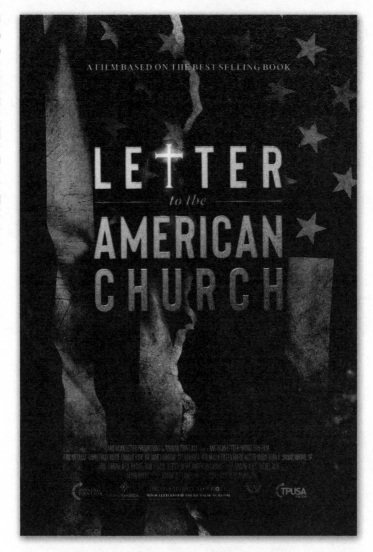

Watch *Letter to the American Church* now! From *New York Times* bestselling author Eric Metaxas comes a riveting new film challenging audiences to take a stand in the face of evil. The striking similarites between the church in early Nazi Germany and the modern American church are chilling and grim.

This is the hour of the American church.

LETTERTOTHEAMERICANCHURCH.COM